# Walking with Jesus

## Bible and Reading for Fourth Grade

**Barbara Keller**

with

**Martha Shirley & Rosemarie Ricciardi**

The Noah Plan®

*Biblical · Classical · American Education*

**Foundation for American Christian Education**

Chesapeake, Virginia

# Walking with Jesus
## Bible and Reading for Fourth Grade

Barbara Keller

with

Martha Shirley & Rosemarie Ricciardi

Copyright © July 2005

FOUNDATION FOR AMERICAN CHRISTIAN EDUCATION

ISBN 0-912498-41-2

Graphic Design,
Desta Garrett

Copyediting,
Sarah Huston

Theological Editing,
Dr. James Arcieri, M.Div., D.Min.

All Scripture references are taken from either the King James Version or the New International Version of the Bible unless otherwise noted.

Cover Art
Peggy Coven, *Walking with Jesus*, 2005
12.5″ x 17.75″ chalk pastel on paper, private collection.
Throughout book: Peggy Coven, *Hand in Hand*, 2005
8.5″ x 11″ pencil on paper, private collection.

Images used in text from
*Egermeier's Bible Story Book* by Elsie E. Egermeier,
originally published by Warner Press in Anderson, Indiana, 1922.

**Published by**

# The Foundation for American Christian Education

*Transforming the Mind and Heart of a Nation*

**PO Box 9588, Chesapeake, Virginia 23321**

**Ordering and catalogue**
**800-352-3223 • www.face.net**

# Acknowledgments

The writing of *Walking with Jesus: Bible and Reading for Fourth Grade* was an act of love shared by three exceptionally gifted and successful teachers of children. Barbara Keller, Martha Shirley, and Rosemarie Ricciardi have a collective classroom experience of eighty-five years in addition to their work as curriculum designers and writers. All three are highly regarded teachers of teachers whose contribution to the practical application of the Principle Approach® is widely appreciated.

The *Walking with Jesus* student book was written by Barbara Keller who carried the vision for imparting to fourth graders through the study of the Bible a sense of the intimacy and wonder of the Christian walk. Martha Shirley, author of *The Noah Plan® Reading Curriculum Guide*, integrated the Bible-as-Reader techniques and strategies into the text and developed the companion *Teacher Planner* charts on CD to guide the teaching of reading hand-in-glove with the Bible study. Rosemarie Ricciardi wrote the teacher direction segment of the *Teacher Planner* CD and collaborated with Martha in designing the reading aspects of the student notebook assignments. The three writers have created a unique and valuable tool for fourth grade teaching and learning—a student book that guides the student in creating a notebook record of the study of the Bible while refining reading skills.

An unusual element of the writing of *Walking with Jesus* is the care given to "test drive" the book. The writing process included the huge project of developing a student notebook as directed by *Walking with Jesus* to test the appropriateness, intensity, and direction given for each student assignment. This step, initiated by Rosemarie Ricciardi and Barbara Keller, enabled the writers to refine assignments, bring more clarity to the directions, and make the text most effective. The result is a fourth grade Bible and reading program that allows the student the opportunity to relish the Bible and reason from its principles while developing advanced reading skills.

The editorial team also included Sarah Huston, managing editor, and Carole Adams, senior editor. Because the curriculum actually lives in the classroom, the work of Nancy Hameloth and Rose Alison, fourth grade teachers at StoneBridge School, helped authenticate the process. Dr. Jim Arcieri, headmaster of Stone-Bridge School, contributed time to review the hermeneutic and theological elements of the book.

We're excited about *Walking with Jesus* and appreciate the inspiration of the Holy Spirit and the vitality and infinite value of the Word of God that enlightens our lives and hearts and establish truth as our base for living. May many thousands of fourth graders grow strong in spirit and mighty in character through the use of this book in the study of the Bible.

# Contents

# List of Pictures

Illustrations in *Walking with Jesus* are taken from *Egermeier's Bible Story Book* by Elsie E. Egermeier published by the Warner Press in Anderson, Indiana.

# *Walking with Jesus*

## Preface

What does it mean to walk with Jesus? What does it look like? The Bible is full of examples of men and women who walked with Him. Their faith and trust in God will encourage and provide a model for you.

You are embarking on a journey through the study of the Bible that will teach you about God. You will learn how to recognize God's providential hand in your life. Additionally, you will refine your reasoning and reading skills as you build your notebook with the study of the Bible. May God bless your journey and give you eyes to see Him.

# Dear Student,

Welcome to *Walking with Jesus*, the study of the Bible in the fourth grade! We will begin each day with praise, with learning the truth of God's Word found in the Bible, and with prayer. Our purpose is to know God and to apply His Word to our lives. In order to do this, we will use certain tools. See the box on page xiv for the supplies you will need.

As we study the Bible, we will see that God values order. God's order is seen in His character, His dealings with men, and the world He has created. The Bible also reveals that God values the making of written records. The first thing we will need to do in preparation for our studies is to set up the notebook. The Bible notebook will contain the permanent record of our study for the year, which includes memory verses, notes on the Bible studies, reason questions, map work, and reading assignments. The Notebook Standard provides the guidelines for the notebook that give it value and usefulness.

## How to Follow the Notebook Standard

1. Prepare a title page for the Bible notebook. See the one modeled for you on the page xiv. Your notebook title page is a representation of your individual character. Enjoy expressing yourself as you draw and color an appropriate illustration. The title page is placed in the front of the notebook.

2. Use block lettering to prepare four dividers with labeled tabs. File the dividers behind the title page.
   - Quarter One
   - Quarter Two
   - Quarter Three
   - Quarter Four

3. File the Bible Overview for fourth grade in front of the dividers behind your title page.

4. The notebook work is done in one color of ink (black or blue) using cursive handwriting, a ruler is used for all drawn lines and charts, and colored pencils for illustrations (no magic markers or gels). The notebook is kept according to the following standards:

- Neatness—Use correct and legible penmanship, make neat corrections, do not doodle in the margins or on the cover (inside or out), and keep your writing out of the margins.

- Accuracy—Divide words correctly at the end of a syllable and correct all errors by drawing a straight line through the error and writing the correction above or beside it.

- Completeness—File all notes and assignments in the notebook.

- Order—File all pages behind the correct divider in order by date.

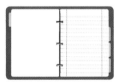 Look for this notebook symbol throughout the book. It always appears beside special notebook instructions.

To remind yourself of the notebook standard necessary to maintain excellence, record the following page that summarizes the Notebook Standard. File this page behind the Bible Overview.

"My Bible Notebook Standard"

- I will use black or blue ink throughout my Bible notebook.

- I will maintain my notebook in the following order: title page, overview, notebook standards, Quarter One, Quarter Two, Quarter Three, and Quarter Four.

- I will observe the following standards in producing my notebook. (Copy the four standards for your notebook listed above—Neatness, Accuracy, Completeness, and Order.)

At the bottom of the page, use colored pencils to draw a small illustration of your Bible notebook.

## Supplies for Bible

* The Adventure Bible (NIV)
* *An American Dictionary of the English Language,* Noah Webster, 1828 facsimile edition
* The Bantam *Roget's Thesaurus*
* Three-ring binder with two-inch rings
* Four dividers with tabs
* Twelve-inch ruler
* Colored pencils
* Blue or black pens

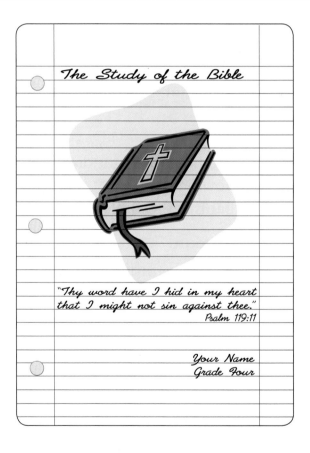

*The Study of the Bible*

*"Thy word have I hid in my heart that I might not sin against thee."*
Psalm 119:11

*Your Name*
*Grade Four*

One of the most important routines you will follow every week is the memorization of the Bible memory verse. Use Webster's 1828 *Dictionary* to define unfamiliar vocabulary and discuss the verse with your teacher or parent. Practice the verse daily in order to commit it to memory for recitation at the end of the week.

Martha Shirley with two fourth grade
StoneBridge School reading students

# The Immediacy of Christ

# Introduction to Studying the Bible

Why study the Bible? Open your Webster's 1828 *Dictionary* and read the definition of *Bible.* From this definition, you can see that the Bible is God's book; it tells us about His character, the principles of the Christian faith, and how we are to live. The Bible says in 2 Timothy 3:16–17 that it was inspired by God so that we might learn truth and how to correct our behavior in order to be useful and prepared for good works.

Read the overview for Bible to see where you are headed in your studies. Notice the theme of the first unit Bible studies, "The Immediacy of Jesus Christ—'the I Am.'" This means that the presence of God upon the earth was revealed to man through the life of Jesus as a man. *Emmanuel*, which means "God with us," is one of the names of Jesus.

Listen as your teacher explains the K-W-L chart and begin this portion of your notebook work before you begin your reading on the deity of Jesus (qualities that show Jesus is God). Learn about the deity of Jesus Christ—God made human—by reading the following Scriptures:

* John 1:1–5
* John 8:27–30
* Matthew 1:16, 20, 23
* Romans 1:3
* Galatians 4:4
* Colossians 1:15–20

*Jesus is the Word made flesh.*

### Discussion and Notebook Work

1. Record the memory verse and file.

   "And the Word was made flesh, and dwelt among us, (and we beheld his glory, the glory as of the only begotten of the Father,) full of grace and truth." (John 1:14)

2. Practice the memory verse to recite at the end of the week.

3. File the **overview** distributed by the teacher.

4. Read 2 Timothy 3:16 and restate the purpose of the Bible in your own words. (This is called *paraphrasing*.)

5. Complete a **K-W-L chart** to engage your thinking before, during, and after reading the above Scriptures. (See sample form on the next page.)

| What I **Know** | What I **Want** to Learn | What I Have **Learned** |
|---|---|---|
| | | |

6. Complete a **concept/definition map** for *deity*. (See sample form, p. 18.)

7. Write a paragraph relating what you have learned about the deity of Jesus.

# How Did the Bible Come to Us?

The Old Testament tells the story of how God revealed Himself to mankind. It was written by people who were inspired by God over the course of nearly one thousand years. God's relationship with the people and the things He told them were handwritten by scribes on scrolls in the Hebrew language. These scrolls were kept in the synagogues (Jewish temples for worship) of Jesus' day and were used to teach the people.

The New Testament writings tell the story of the early church after Jesus came to earth and were written by Christians of Jesus' day in the Greek language. The New Testament is often called the *Gospel* (or "good news") of Jesus Christ.

Over time, scholars translated these writings into the languages of other peoples. There was a Latin translation in 410 A.D. called the *Vulgate*. The first English Bible was translated in 1384 A.D. by John Wycliffe, who was called "the Morning Star of the Reformation." In 1456, John Gutenberg made the distribution of the Bible easier with the invention of the printing press. The first book he printed was a Latin Bible. As time went on, more translations were produced at the cost of much persecution of those who wanted to make the Bible available to everyone. The Geneva Bible was produced in Switzerland in 1560 and was the Bible the Pilgrims brought to America. The King James Version of 1611 was an English translation commissioned by King James I of England, which became one of the most popular Bibles of all time because of the beauty and excellence of its written expression. Its popularity continues to this day even with so many new Bible translations.

There is more and more evidence being discovered to document the authenticity of the Bible as archeologists uncover parchments and fragments of the books of the Bible. The Dead Sea Scrolls were one such discovery: they

*Jesus is the Word made flesh.*

were found in a cave in Israel in 1947 and contained the book of Isaiah and parts of all the other Old Testament books except Esther.

## Early Bible Translations

| | | |
|---|---|---|
| Paul | Wycliffe | The |
| Christian Church | First English Bible | Pilgrims |
| 50 | 1384 | 1620 |

Jesus          410          1456      1560      1611
              Latin        Gutenberg  Geneva   King James
              Vulgate      Bible      Bible    Bible

### *Discussion and Notebook Work*

1. Use your Bible dictionary-concordance to record the definition for *scribe*.

2. Record the **timeline** of the different translations of the Bible.

3. Use a **T-chart** to compare and contrast passages Psalm 23 and 2 Timothy 3:16 in the King James Version and the Adventure Bible (or another version) using the following example.

| | King James | Adventure Bible |
|---|---|---|
| *Psalm 23* | | |
| *v. 1* | *"The LORD is my shepherd; I shall not want."* | *". . . I shall not be in want."* |
| *v. 2* | | |

4. Write a paragraph explaining why it is important for every person to have his own Bible and what your Bible has meant to you.

# The Divisions of the Bible

Much more could be said about the history of the Bible, and in praise of its high quality of literary expression and its power to change lives, but let's jump in and familiarize ourselves with the parts of the Bible. Open your Bible to the front and examine the Contents page. Do you see the list of the books divided into the Old Testament and the New Testament? You may have already learned the divisions of the Bible. If so, this will be a great review for you! There are four major divisions of the Old Testament and New Testament:

Jesus is the Word made flesh.

## The Sixty-Six Books of the Bible

| Old Testament (39 books) | New Testament (27 books) |
| --- | --- |
| 1. The Pentateuch or the Law (Genesis, Exodus, Leviticus, Numbers, and Deuteronomy) | 1. The Gospels (Matthew, Mark, Luke, and John) |
| 2. History (Joshua, Judges, Ruth, 1 & 2 Samuel, 1 & 2 Kings, 1 & 2 Chronicles, Ezra, Nehemiah, and Esther) | 2. History (Acts or Acts of the Apostles) |
| 3. Poetry or Wisdom (Job, Psalms, Proverbs, Song of Solomon, and Ecclesiastes) | 3. The Epistles (Romans, 1 & 2 Corinthians, Galatians, Ephesians, Philippians, Colossians, 1 & 2 Thessalonians, 1 & 2 Timothy, Titus, Philemon, Hebrews, James, 1 & 2 Peter, 1–3 John, and Jude) |
| 4. Prophecy <br> ★ Major Prophets—Isaiah, Jeremiah, Lamentations, Ezekiel, Daniel <br> ★ Minor Prophets—Hosea, Joel, Amos, Obadiah, Jonah, Micah, Nahum, Habakkuk, Zephaniah, Haggai, Zechariah, and Malachi | 4. Prophecy (Revelation) |

### Discussion and Notebook Work

1. Use Webster's 1828 *Dictionary* to record the definition for *testament*.
2. Record and file the above chart showing the four major divisions of the Old Testament and the New Testament in your notebook.

# Making Good Use of Your Bible

You should be very familiar with your Bible, since it will be a source of wisdom for you in every subject you study this year and every day of your life. Examine the pages after the Contents page in the Adventure

**The Immediacy of Christ**

Bible and then look at the back of your Bible to locate the Index, Activities, Dictionary-Concordance, and Maps. To practice using your Bible, follow the directions below and record your work. (If you are using another version of the Bible, practice locating and using the features of that Bible.)

### Discussion and Notebook Work

1. Use your Bible dictionary-concordance to record the definition for *doctrine*. Choose a verse where the word is found and record it.

2. Use the index in your Bible to find information about the animals of the Bible. Turn to one of the pages listed. Summarize the new information you learned about one of the animals from your reading.

3. Turn to the Activities section in the back of your Bible and find "Do an Experiment." Follow the directions in the special feature, "Let's Live It: Hard Heart, Soft Heart" and record the results.

4. Reason and relate by describing a time when God's Word made a difference in your actions.

# The Great "I Am"
### Exodus 3; John 8; Revelation 4

Remember, according to the overview, the theme for this unit's study is "The Immediacy of Christ." Do you remember what this means? If not, go back to the previous lesson to review what you learned.

Read the memory verse for this week (Revelation 1:8) and notice the words *Alpha* and *Omega*, followed by the words the *beginning* and the *ending*. These words stand for the first and the last letters of the Greek alphabet. Then the Lord says, "which is, and which was, and which is to come, the Almighty." The Lord is saying "I Am the eternal God" and "I Am Lord over the past, present, and future." Another way of saying this is Jesus is the eternal, self-existing Lord. *I Am* is a title indicating self-existence (*Self-existence* means that God doesn't need anything but Himself to be [He doesn't need food or a place to live or air to breathe like we do].). Jesus is the Creator. He was not created and has no beginning or end. This means He is eternal. If you don't quite understand, ask your teacher or parent to explain this more fully.

To further explore this topic, turn in your Bible and read Exodus 3:14, John 8:58–59, and Revelation 4:8.

### Discussion and Notebook Work

1. Record the memory verse and file.

   "I am Alpha and Omega, the beginning and the ending, saith the Lord, which is, and which was, and which is to come, the Almighty." (Revelation 1:8)

2. Practice the memory verse to recite at the end of the week.

3. After reading the verses in Exodus, John, and Revelation, reason and discuss why you think the Jews picked up stones to stone Jesus.

4. Look at the **cause-and-effect graphic organizer** below to focus on the relationship in which Jesus' words (cause) brought certain events about (effects) and record it in your notebook.

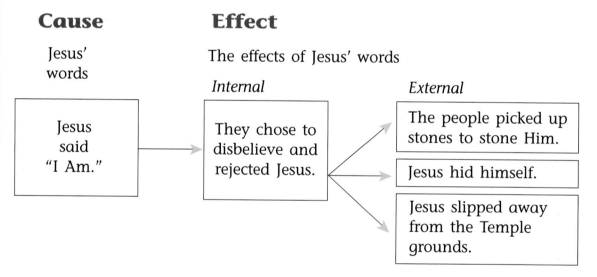

| Cause | Effect |

5. Use the information on the **cause-and-effect graphic organizer** to record your thoughts about the actions of the Jews and the actions of Jesus.

# The "I Am's" of Scripture
## John; Revelation

The New Testament books of John, the First, Second, and Third Epistles of John, and Revelation were written by John, who referred to himself as "the disciple whom Jesus loved." His writings repeatedly reveal the deity of Jesus Christ. Now read the following Scriptures from the Gospel of John and the book of Revelation to learn other things Jesus reveals about Himself. Complete the chart modeled below as you read the following passages.

- ★ John 6:35–58
- ★ John 10:1–9
- ★ John 10:11
- ★ John 10:36
- ★ John 11:25
- ★ John 13:13
- ★ John 14:6
- ★ John 15:1–8
- ★ Revelation 22:16

### Discussion and Notebook Work

1. Use a ruler to create and complete a page like the following one as you read and think about the Scriptures.

#### The "I Am's" of Scripture

| Scripture Passage | Name of Jesus | Meaning |
|---|---|---|
| John 6:35-58 | Bread of Life | Jesus gives spiritual food and eternal life. |
| John 10:1-9 | | |
| | | |
| | | |

2. Summarize in a paragraph what you have learned about God by studying the "I Am's" of Jesus.

# Other Names for Jesus
### Selected Scriptures

Jesus reveals Himself as God.

You have learned some of the names Jesus used in speaking about Himself. Your Webster's 1828 *Dictionary* defines the noun *name*: "In Scripture the name of God signifies his titles, his attributes, his will or purpose, his honor and glory, his word, his grace, his wisdom, power and goodness, his worship or service, or God himself."

An *attribute* of God is something that is part of His character or belongs to Him. Read the following Scriptures to learn more about the attributes of Jesus:

* Isaiah 9:6
* John 1:29, 36
* Ephesians 2:19–20
* 1 Timothy 6:14–15
* Revelation 5:5

### Discussion and Notebook Work

1. Create a page and record the Scripture references and the new names you learned for Jesus.

### Names of Jesus Revealing His Attributes

| Scripture Verses | Names of Jesus |
|---|---|
| *Isaiah 9:6–"For to us a child is born, to us a son is given, and the government will be on his shoulders. And he will be called Wonderful Counselor, Mighty God, Everlasting Father, Prince of Peace."* | * *Wonderful Counselor* <br> * <br> * <br> * |
| *John 1:29, 36* | * |
| *Ephesians 2:19–20* | * |
| *1 Timothy 6:14–15* | * <br> * <br> * <br> * |
| *Revelation 5:5* | * <br> * |

2. Write a paragraph stating the Biblical view and the importance of a name.

# Jesus Calls Individuals

Remember the "I Am's" of last week's lessons. You learned that *the Immediacy of Christ* is the presence of God upon the earth revealed to man through the life of Jesus among us. You learned about His character and relationship with man. The fact is, Jesus loves us and has a purpose for our lives. Last week's lesson revealed that He wants to be our Master and Lord. That involves each of us accepting Him as our own Savior and obeying His call to follow Him as we each live our lives. To understand this better, you will need to define the following words from Webster's 1828 *Dictionary*: *call, disciple, discipleship,* and *training*. You will read the definitions to apply them to our topic. Though all the definitions will help you get a sense of the meaning, some are closer than others for our purposes. Identify which definition best relates to our topic ("Jesus Calls Individuals"). To help you get started, here are some hints from the definitions for two of the words:

* Pay particular attention to definition ten for the word *call*.

* The second definition of *disciple* applies to our lesson.

### Discussion and Notebook Work

1. Record the memory verse and file.

   "For my mouth shall speak truth; and wickedness is an abomination to my lips. All the words of my mouth are in righteousness; there is nothing froward or perverse in them." (Proverbs 8:7–8)

2. Practice the memory verses to recite at the end of the week.

3. Record the applicable definitions for *call, disciple, discipleship,* and *training*.

4. Write sentences to demonstrate your understanding of the words as they relate to the call of Jesus.

# Jesus Calls the Twelve Disciples
## Selected Scriptures

Jesus calls disciples and equips them for service and ministry.

Jesus called twelve disciples, whom he taught and trained to do the work of the ministry and to follow Him. As you study each of their lives and call, you may identify with their struggles and see yourself through their lives. Study the passages about each disciple to identify what can be learned about each man and record the information. Use the chart under Discussion and Notebook Work.

Simon Peter
* Matthew 4:18–20; 16:21–23; 18:21–22
* John 1:41–42; 21:15–17
* Luke 5:5–11

Andrew
* Matthew 4:18–20
* John 1:40–42; 6:8–9

John
* Matthew 4:21–22; 10:1–2
* Mark 1:19
* Luke 9:49–50, 54–55

James
* Matthew 4:21–22; 10:1–2
* Luke 9:54–55

Philip
* John 1:43–48; 6:5–7; 14:8–12
* Matthew 10:3

Nathanael
* John 1:45–51

Matthew
* Luke 5:27–28
* Mark 2:14

Thomas
* Matthew 10:3
* John 14:1–6; 20:25–29

Judas Iscariot
* John 12:4–6
* Luke 6:13–16

Simon the Zealot
* Matthew 10:2–4

Thaddaeus (known as the brother of James the Younger)
* Matthew 10:2–3

James the Younger
* Matthew 10:2–4
* Matthew 27:56
* Mark 15:40
* Acts 1:13

## Discussion and Notebook Work

1. Create a page similar to the one below and record the information you have learned from your reading about each disciple. The first disciple, Simon Peter, has been done for you as an example.

### Jesus Calls the Twelve Disciples

| Disciple | The Call and Individuality of This Disciple |
|---|---|
| Simon Peter | Matthew 4:18–20 (responded at once to the call of Jesus) <br> Matthew 16:21–23 (rebuked Jesus) <br> Matthew 18:21–22 (asked Jesus questions) <br> John 1:41–42 (name changed) <br> John 21:15 (restored to Jesus and given a task) <br> Luke 5:5–11 (was obedient) <br> Acts 10 (taught Gentiles) |
| Andrew | |

2. Tell how the disciples demonstrated voluntary consent in following Jesus.

3. Record which disciple you relate to the most and why.

# Jesus Trains Those He Calls
## Matthew 10

Jesus calls disciples and equips them for service and ministry.

Wouldn't it have been wonderful to know Jesus, to learn from Him directly, and to be called His friends like Peter, James, John, and the others? Guess what—you may not be able to see Him with your eyes, but we have the Word of God (the Bible), and His Spirit in us to teach us! The Word says He will never leave or forsake us (Deuteronomy 31:6–8, Joshua 1:5, Hebrews 13:5). So, unlike the disciples, we are always in His presence. Remember, the presence of God on the earth is called *the Immediacy of Christ.*

Part of our discipleship as Christians is to submit to being trained in how we are to live in relationship to God and to others. You defined the key words *call, disciple, discipleship,* and *training* in the last lesson. Reread those definitions from your notebook in preparation for this lesson.

The New Testament has many examples of Jesus teaching or training His disciples. You will learn some of what the disciples were taught through your reading. Read Matthew 10:1 describing how Jesus equipped the twelve.

### Discussion and Notebook Work

1. Record the memory verse and file.

   "They are all plain to him that understandeth, and right to them that find knowledge. Receive my instruction, and not silver; and knowledge rather than choice gold." (Proverbs 8:9–10)

2. Practice the memory verses to recite at the end of the week.

3. Complete a **word map** for *disciple.*

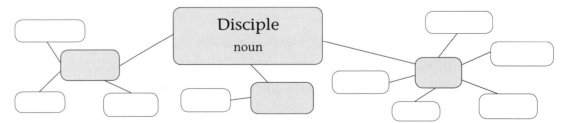

Disciple
noun

4. Write a summary of how Jesus equipped the twelve disciples from your reading.

5. Write a paragraph about what it means to be a disciple of Jesus.

# Specific Instructions for the Twelve
## Matthew 10

Those God has placed in authority over you will instruct you in how to behave wisely and how to be successful in accomplishing your goals. Your parents, teachers, and pastor are primarily those who are responsible for this at this time in your life. Later on in your life, the list of those who will speak words of instruction to you may include your boss, co-workers, your spouse, and friends. Read the following to learn about some specific instructions Jesus gave the disciples:

⋆ Jesus instructs the twelve before they went out (Matthew 10:5–15).
⋆ Jesus tells them how to deal with persecution (Matthew 10:16–23).

*Jesus calls disciples and equips them for service and ministry.*

### Discussion and Notebook Work

1. Use your Bible dictionary-concordance to record the definition for *authority*. Read the related Scriptures.
2. Rephrase in your own words the instructions Jesus gave to the twelve about how they were to go out.
3. Summarize in a paragraph what Jesus told the disciples to do when they were persecuted.

# Some Hard Teaching
## Matthew 10

In the passages you are about to read, there are some hard teachings that should cause you to think carefully about your commitment to follow the Lord. In Matthew 10:38 Jesus told the disciples, "anyone who does not take his cross and follow me is not worthy of me." The passage indicates that

*The disciples were chosen by Jesus to tell others about Him.*

there will be hardship and suffering, and that you must be willing to leave everything to follow him. Read the following passages and discuss with your teacher anything you don't understand:

★ The student is not above his master (Matthew 10:24–33)
★ Family relationships (Matthew 10:34–39)

### Discussion and Notebook Work

1. Use your Webster's 1828 *Dictionary* to record the definition for *commitment*.

2. Write a sentence to demonstrate your understanding of the word *commitment*.

3. Reason and relate by writing a paragraph telling what you think would be the most difficult teaching for you in your reading today.

# Reward for Right Behavior
## Matthew 10

To conclude this week's lesson, read Matthew 10:40–42. Pay particular attention to the things Jesus says bring a reward.

### Discussion and Notebook Work

1. Record and answer the reason questions.

   a. When Jesus calls me to be His disciple, does my individuality affect the call?

   b. Compare the individuality of the disciples you studied. How are they alike and different? (You may need to look back to your work from the previous lesson.)

   c. When Jesus calls us to follow Him, will our training always be the same as other people's? Explain.

2. Complete a **word wheel** for *reward* using the following steps.

   ★ List and label synonyms and antonyms for reward.

   | Synonym | Antonym |
   |---------|---------|
   | 1. Payment | Punishment |
   | 2. | |
   | 3. | |

   ★ Fill in the **word wheel** with synonyms and antonyms.

   ★ Label the synonyms and the antonyms.

God's Principle of Individuality

Jesus calls disciples and equips them for service and ministry.

# The Beatitudes
## Matthew 5

Do you want your life to be happy and blessed? All people would probably answer yes to that question. But do all people do the things that will bring happiness and blessing into their lives? Most definitely, the answer is no. You see, God has designed the world with physical laws (like

Blessings come from following Jesus' Word.

gravity) that affect our lives whether we want them to or not. For instance, if you jump off of the top of a ten-story building without a parachute, you will most likely die because the law of gravity will cause you to come crashing to the ground. God also ordained spiritual laws that bring blessing if you obey them and unpleasant consequences if you do not obey them. For instance, the Bible says in Exodus 20:12, "Honor your father and your mother, so that you may live long in the land the LORD your God is giving you." This implies that if you do not honor your mother and father, you may not live as long as you would like.

When Jesus was on the earth, He taught virtues that He wanted to see developed in the lives of His followers. Some of these teachings are in the portion of Scripture from Jesus' Sermon on the Mount called *the beatitudes*. The word *beatitude* comes from the Latin words for "happy," "to bless," and "to make." The beatitudes are a guide for all believers that show which behaviors will bring a blessing upon their lives. They may be hard to understand because they contradict how we usually behave without Jesus' help.

### *Discussion and Notebook Work*

1. Record the memory verses and file.

   "Blessed are the poor in spirit: for theirs is the kingdom of heaven. Blessed are they that mourn: for they shall be comforted. Blessed are the meek: for they shall inherit the earth. Blessed are they which do hunger and thirst after righteousness: for they shall be filled. Blessed are the merciful: for they shall obtain mercy." (Matthew 5:3–7)

2. Practice the memory verses to recite at the end of the week.

3. Complete a **concept/definition map** for *beatitude*.

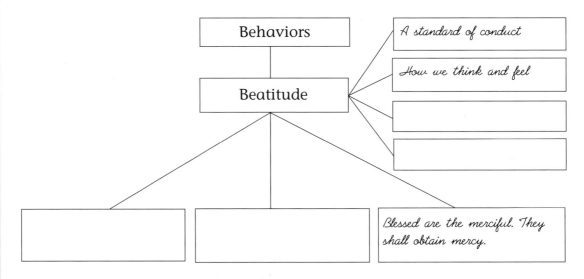

Concept/Definition Map

(1) What are some examples?

(2) My sentence(s):

_____

_____

4. Draw from your own experience to write a paragraph describing how the internal attitude of a person is revealed by a person's external behavior.

# The Origin of Attitudes
## Matthew 5

**A**re you familiar with the Scripture that says, "For as he thinketh in his heart so is he"? (Proverbs 23:7a) The attitude (internal thinking or emotions) of a person is revealed by his external behavior. Jesus' words can change our hearts and minds if we are willing. Then our behavior will line up with correct thinking. Romans 12:2 says, "Do not conform any longer to the pattern of this world, but be transformed by the renewing of your mind. Then you will be able to test and approve what God's will is—his good, pleasing and perfect will." Turn in your Bible to Matthew 5:3–10 and read the beatitudes.

### *Discussion and Notebook Work*

1. Create and complete a page on the beatitudes as you do the reading.

## The Beatitudes

| Scripture | Worldly View | Kingdom View | Blessing |
|-----------|--------------|--------------|----------|
| Poor in spirit (Matthew 5:3) | Independent of God | Dependent on God | Kingdom of heaven |
| Mournful (Matthew 5:4) | | Sorry for sin | |
| Meek (Matthew 5:5) | Disobedient | Strength under control | Inherit the blessings of earth |
| Hungry and thirsty (Matthew 5:7) | | Desire for righteousness | |
| Merciful (Matthew 5:7) | | Undeserved tenderness and kindness | |
| Pure in heart (Matthew 5:8) | | Free from guilt | |
| Peacemaker (Matthew 5:9) | | Mediator, intercessor | |
| Persecuted (Matthew 5:10) | | Suffer for doing what is right | |

# Luke's Version of the Beatitudes
## Matthew 5; Luke 6

The beatitudes are a guide for all believers.

The book of Luke also includes a portion of the beatitudes from Jesus' Sermon on the Mount. It is not exactly the same as the account in Matthew. Some say Luke's version may be a record of Jesus' teaching on another occasion. Read Luke 6:17–26.

### Discussion and Notebook Work

1. Compare the versions of the beatitudes found in Matthew and Luke. Tell how they are alike and how they are different using a page like the one below.

| The Beatitudes | Matthew 5:1–12 | Luke 6:17–26 |
| --- | --- | --- |
| Setting | | |
| Characters | | |
| Events | | |

# The Sermon on the Mount
## Matthew 22

The two greatest commandments

In the last lesson, you studied a portion of Scripture called the beatitudes. Review by reciting the memory verses you learned. You may remember that the beatitudes are part of a larger portion of Scripture called the Sermon on the Mount. On a hillside near Capernaum, Jesus taught His disciples many practical things about living in God's kingdom. Read Matthew 22:37–40 and think about the two greatest commandments. Keep them in the back of your mind as you study the Sermon on the Mount and think about how all of the Lord's instructions are actually summed up in these two commands.

### Discussion and Notebook Work

1. Record the memory verses and file.

   "Blessed are the pure in heart: for they shall see God. Blessed are the peacemakers: for they shall be called the children of God. Blessed are they which are persecuted for righteousness' sake: for theirs is the kingdom of heaven. Blessed are ye, when men shall revile you, and persecute you, and shall say all manner of evil against you falsely, for my sake. Rejoice, and be exceeding glad: for great is your reward in heaven: for so persecuted they the prophets which were before you."

   (Matthew 5:8–12)

2. Practice the memory verses to recite at the end of the week.

3. Use your Bible dictionary-concordance to record the definition for *commandment*.

   ⋆ Read the related Scriptures.
   ⋆ Use the word in a sentence relating it to the lesson.

4. Complete a **Venn diagram** to compare and contrast the two greatest commandments. (See the chart below.)

#### The Two Greatest Commandments

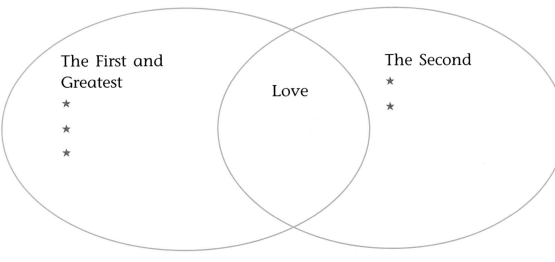

The First and Greatest
⋆
⋆
⋆

Love

The Second
⋆
⋆

5. Write a paragraph relating a time when you loved your neighbor as yourself.

# The Teaching Style of Jesus
## Matthew 5; Colossians 4

Jesus was a very skillful teacher who was able to relate to His disciples through word pictures, parables, and illustrations from life that everyone could understand. That is why the Bible translates to all cultures. Read the metaphor found in Matthew 5:13. Remember, a *metaphor* is a figure of speech that uses language normally applied to one object and uses it to refer to something else. Matthew 5:13 compares the Christian to salt. As you know, salt is a seasoning used to flavor food. It is also a preservative, which was particularly valuable before refrigeration. Read Colossians 4:6. Realize that if we are to be salt in our world, standing against sin, we must have the characteristics of the kingdom which will draw men to Christ, the living Word. Salt also makes people thirsty.

### Discussion and Notebook Work

1. Complete a **concept/definition map** for *parable*.

2. Record the questions below. Reason and relate to complete your answers.

   a. What does Matthew 5:13 imply about a Christian who is not salty?

   b. What influence on the world will a Christian have if he is not salty?

   c. Explain how you think your conversation could be seasoned with salt as stated in Colossians 4:6.

# The Light of the World
## Matthew 5; John 8

In Matthew 5:14–16, Christians are compared to light. As you know, light drives out darkness. Remember John 8:12 says, "I am the light of the world:

The Immediacy of Christ

he that followeth me shall not walk in darkness, but shall have the light of life."

## Discussion and Notebook Work

1. Use your Bible dictionary-concordance to record the definition for *light*.

2. Find and record other Scriptures which refer to Jesus as the Light of the world.

3. Underline the metaphors in the Scriptures you have written that identify Jesus as the light of the world.

4. Record the questions below. Reason and relate to complete the answers.
   a. What did Jesus overcome when He died on the cross for us?
   b. Give examples of how you can let your light shine at school, at home, and in your community without drawing attention to yourself.

# Identifying False Prophets
## Matthew 7

In the last study, you learned that because of the salt and light in lives of true Christians, those Christians influence their world. Matthew 7:15–23 warns that there are some people who pretend to be Christians. The passage describes the good tree and the bad tree. Although we are not to judge others, we are warned to be careful to not listen to pretenders called *false prophets*. Read the passage carefully to learn how to identify false prophets.

God has given us standards by which to guide our lives.

## Discussion and Notebook Work

1. Discuss the characteristics of an imitator and pretender (or false prophet). Record two or three ways to know false prophets.

2. Use a **picture graph** to illustrate the two metaphors studied—the good tree and the bad tree.

3. Explain what you think the following expression means: a "wolf in sheep's clothing."

# Jesus Is Our Advocate
## Selected Scriptures

As we continue to study "The Immediacy of Christ," we learn this week that Jesus is our *Advocate*. This is a word that is probably unfamiliar to you, so you will need to research the definition in your Webster's 1828 *Dictionary*. From the definition you see that an advocate is necessary in a court of law. There is a heavenly court room, so to speak, in which only Jesus can represent us before our heavenly Father. First John 2:1 tells us why: "My little children, these things write I unto you, that ye sin not. And if any man sin, we have an advocate with the father, Jesus Christ the righteous." Learn this passage for your memory verse this week as you study other Scriptures that reveal more about Jesus, our Advocate.

### Discussion and Notebook Work

1. Record your memory verse and file.

   "My little children, these things write I unto you, that ye sin not. And if any man sin, we have an advocate with the Father, Jesus Christ the righteous." (1 John 2:1)

2. Practice the memory verse to recite at the end of the week.

3. Complete a **concept/definition map** for the noun *advocate* using your Webster's 1828 *Dictionary* and your Bible dictionary-concordance.

4. Use a ruler to create and complete a page like the one below as you read the passages that describe Jesus as our Advocate and briefly record what you learn.

### Jesus Is Our Advocate[1]

| Why Is Jesus Our Advocate? | How Does Jesus Defend Believers? | What Blessings Have Been Bestowed upon Believers? | What Has Jesus Equipped Us to Do? |
|---|---|---|---|
| John 15:16 *Jesus chose us.* | Luke 22:31–34 | 2 Corinthians 5:21 | Matthew 28:19–20 |
| Revelation 1:5 | Hebrews 13:6 | John 20:22 *Jesus gave us another comforter—the Holy Spirit.* | 2 Corinthians 5:18–20 |
| Colossians 1:27 | Psalm 23:1 | John 15:15 | Matthew 16:19 |
| | 2 Timothy 4:17–18 | | Luke 10:19 *We are given power to overcome Satan.* |
| | | | James 5:14 |

5. Write a paragraph to summarize what you learned about one of the questions from the above chart.

# Jesus Is Our Intercessor
## John 17

As you continue to study the Bible as a disciple of Christ, you will learn much about the character of Jesus and who He is to us. Today's lesson reveals Jesus as our *Intercessor*. The word may be familiar to you, but research the definition in your Webster's 1828 *Dictionary* to clarify the meaning of *intercessor*. You may also need to define other words in the definition like *mediator, interpose,* and *reconcile*. From the definitions you learn that an intercessor is someone who argues on behalf of another. Did you realize that Jesus is doing this for you to the Father?

Jesus is our Intercessor.

### *Discussion and Notebook Work*

1. Record your memory verse and file it.

   "But he was wounded for our transgressions, he was bruised for our iniquities: the chastisement of our peace was upon him; and with his stripes we are healed." (Isaiah 53:5)

2. Practice the memory verse to recite later in the week.

3. Complete a **word map** for *intercessor*.

4. Write sentences to demonstrate your understanding of the vocabulary: *intercessor, mediator, interpose,* and *reconcile*.

# The Purposes for Intercession in Scripture
## 1 Kings 17; Job 4; Romans 10

Now that you have learned the definition for *intercessor*, you may be able to think back on times when you have needed an intercessor. You may remember a time when you needed your mom to intercede on your behalf with your father. Maybe you needed a parent to intercede on your behalf with your teacher about an issue at school. Perhaps you needed an adult to intercede between you and another young person when you were arguing.

In the Scriptures, you will find other situations that require intercession. Read the following passages: 1 Kings 17:17–24, Job 42:8–10, and Romans 10:1–4. You will find three purposes for intercession revealed in them.

### Discussion and Notebook Work

1. Use Webster's 1828 *Dictionary* to record the definition for *intercession*.

2. Write a paragraph to summarize the purposes for intercession you found in your Scripture reading.

3. Relate how you could be an intercessor.

# Willing Vessels for Intercession
## Selected Scriptures

Maybe you think it takes a special person to be an intercessor. The Scriptures reveal otherwise. All Christians are called to intercede for others. In 1 Timothy 2:1–2 we are taught the following, "I urge, then, first of all, that requests, prayers, intercession, and thanksgiving be

*The Immediacy of Christ*

made for everyone—for kings and all those in authority, that we may live peaceful and quiet lives in all godliness and holiness." Sometimes God will give a person a special assignment in prayer for a particular situation. He may even give you a concern for a particular person or situation to show you that He wants you to intercede in prayer. Obey the Holy Spirit if God touches your heart in this way and you will experience a special blessing as you see God bring the answer.

Read the following examples of intercession: Exodus 34:8–9, 2 Kings 4:32–35, Esther 5:5–7, Nehemiah 1:3–6, and Isaiah 38:1–8.

### Discussion and Notebook Work

1. Write one or two sentences to briefly summarize each passage you read above.

2. Complete a **vocabulary word analysis chart** for *pray* like the one below.

**Pray**

| | |
|---|---|
| 1. Part of Speech: | Verb |
| 2. Etymology: | Hebrew  Latin |
| 3. Definition: | |
| 4. It also means: | |
| 5. Synonym: | |
| 6. Antonym: | |
| 7. Homonym: | |
| 8. Write a sentence using the word: | |

# The Intercessions of Jesus
## John 17

Remember that we began the week by identifying Jesus as our Intercessor. Romans 8:34 says, "Who is he that condemns? Christ Jesus, who died—more than that, who was raised to life—is at the right hand of God and is also interceding for us." Even now, Jesus is praying for us. There are passages in Scripture that record some of the intercessions of Jesus while He was living on earth as a human. Read the following Scriptures to determine whom Jesus interceded for and what His requests were in each passage: John 17:1–5, John 17:6–19, and John 17:20–26.

### Discussions and Notebook Work

1. Use Webster's 1828 *Dictionary* and your Bible dictionary-concordance to record the definitions for *petition*. Notice how the part of speech changes the meaning of the word.

2. Write sentences using *petition* as a noun and as a verb.

3. Create and complete a page like the one below to record the information you have learned from your reading about the intercessions of Jesus.

#### Intercessions of Jesus

| Scriptures | People Jesus Interceded for | Petition |
|---|---|---|
| John 17:1–5 | | |
| John 17:6–19 | *Disciples* | |
| John 17:20–26 | | • *To protect*<br>• *To make them holy*<br>• *To make them one with God*<br>• *To bring them to heaven to see Jesus' glory* |

4. Use Jesus' model of intercession to write a prayer for yourself, your family, and your friends.

# The Geography of the Holy Land

A s we study the Bible over the course of the year, we must understand that God created the earth as the stage for man's activities. Therefore, it is necessary for us to take dominion of the earth, as commanded in Genesis 1:28, by studying the divisions on the earth's surface. To understand the land where Jesus lived, look carefully at a map of the Holy Land in New Testament times. Locate the following places on the map and see if you remember the key events associated with them:

* Bethlehem—this is the town where Jesus was born.

* Bethany—this is the town where Martha, Mary, and Lazarus lived.

* Cana—Jesus turned water into wine at a wedding here.

* Capernaum—Jesus' base of ministry was in this city in northern Galilee.

* Emmaus—Jesus appeared to two disciples after the crucifixion on the road to this town.

* Jerusalem—Jesus appeared to the apostles in the upper room in Jerusalem and commanded and enabled them to spread the good news of the Gospel.

* Nazareth—this was the town where Jesus grew up.

* The Sea of Galilee—several of the disciples fished in this sea and Jesus walked on it.

* Jordan River—this is the major river of Israel that flows from the mountains in the north into the Dead Sea in the south. John baptized Jesus in it.

* Dead Sea (Salt Sea)—the Jordan River flows into the Dead Sea; because it has no outlet, it is so salty that nothing can live in it.

* Mediterranean Sea (The Great Sea)—it is the large sea west of Israel.

Review the map standard before you begin your map and ask the teacher any questions you may have about completing it.

### Discussion and Notebook Work

1. Record the memory verse and file.

   "How beautiful upon the mountains are the feet of him that bringeth good tidings, that publisheth peace; that bringeth good tidings of good, that publisheth salvation; that saith unto Zion, Thy God reigneth!" (Isaiah 52:7)

2. Practice the verse for recitation at the end of the week.

3. Discuss with the teacher the difference between a physical map and a political map.

4. Complete a map of Israel in New Testament times by identifying the political and physical sites from the lesson above on your map.

---

[1] The material for this chart was drawn from: Thomas Nelson Inc., The Open Bible. Nashville, TN: Thomas Nelson Publishers, 1975, 32.

The Immediacy of Christ

# Old Testament History

# Introduction to Old Testament History
## Genesis 1

This unit we will study Old Testament history. In the last unit, you learned that this portion of the Bible is a record of God's revelation of Himself to mankind and the history of His relationship with man. Take a look at your Bible Overview to discover the content of our studies for the next nine weeks.

God is the Creator and the Source of all that exists.

Let's begin with the beginning. Turn in your Webster's 1828 *Dictionary* and read the definitions for *beginning*. From this definition, it is clear that God is the first Cause, Source, or Origin of everything that exists. You may remember from previous studies that the Lord calls Himself the Alpha and Omega, the beginning and the ending (Revelation 1:8). In the first book of the Bible, we learn that, "In the beginning God created the heaven and earth." (Genesis 1:1) The first chapter of Genesis goes on to describe God's creation of the universe. His ultimate creation is described in Genesis 1:26–27. Read these familiar verses. As you look at God's creation, you will discover you were made special, unlike the other creatures God made. You were made in the image of God. Only human beings are created in His image.

In Genesis 1:28, God gave man dominion to use and care for all things in His creation. *Dominion* means to have supreme authority over something. In your Bible, *subdue* is used instead of the word *dominion*. *Subdue* means "to bring under control or to conquer." Only God has absolute rule and authority over the earth. God gave some of His authority to man. This is called the *dominion mandate*. With this ruling comes a responsibility. Man is responsible to understand the laws of creation and to conserve the property of God's handiwork.

**Dominion mandate**

### *Discussion and Notebook Work*

1. Record the memory verse and file.

   "I am the Alpha and Omega, the beginning and the ending." (Revelation 1:8a)

2. Practice the memory verse to recite at the end of the week.

3. Record the definition for *beginning* from the Webster's 1828 *Dictionary*.

4. Record the following questions. Reason to complete the answers and file in your notebook:

   a. What was the greatest of work of all God's creation and why?
   b. Record the things God told man to have dominion over.

5. Create and complete a page similar to the one below on your responsibilities of stewardship at home, at school, and at church.

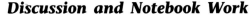

My Stewardship

| Areas | Responsibilities |
|---|---|
| Home | |
| School | |
| Church | |

**God's Principle of Individuality**

6. Read the special feature "Let's Live It: You're Special" from Genesis, chapter one in your Bible and relate it to God's Principle of Individuality. (If you are using another version of the Bible, there may be notes in the margins or other special features you can use.)

# The Fall
## Genesis 3

The first link on the Christian history timeline is Creation. This link is to remind us that God created the world and the other events associated with this time period. These events tell us about who God is and who we are. We need to understand that God is not only Creator, but Sovereign Ruler over all He has created. He has the right to rule over all created things, because they are His property. This includes man, who was made in His image.

In God's goodness, He created everything necessary for life on earth and placed Adam and Eve in a beautiful garden. God gave a command to Adam and Eve: the command is found in Genesis 2:16–17. God's command to them allowed for *free will*, or the choice to obey or disobey. We refer to this as *self-government*.

The following is a brief account of an event that has affected all of God's creation. Adam and Eve had a blessed and peaceful life and a wonderful relationship with God until one sad day. You probably know the story of Adam and Eve's sin of rebellion against God and how the serpent deceived them. This is called *the Fall*. Because they believed the serpent's lie, they made a choice that brought the corruption of sin to all God had created. Man rejected God's command. Review by reading Genesis three, looking for the consequences to Adam, Eve, and the serpent due to their sin.

Let's give particular notice to Genesis 3:14–15. God cursed the serpent and put enmity (hatred) between his offspring and the woman's (mankind). "He will crush your head and you will strike his heel" is a prophecy referring to the coming Savior, Jesus Christ, who would crush and defeat Satan. We see a glimpse of God's love and provision of salvation for mankind from the beginning.

> God is the Creator and Source of everything that exists.
>
> Christian self-government

### Discussion and Notebook Work

1. Read and discuss the definition of *sovereign* in your Bible dictionary-concordance.

2. Use a **cause-and-effect organizer** to understand and record the relationship between the actions of mankind and the serpent (the causes), and the consequences (effects) as you read Genesis three. (See the model chart on the next page.)

| Cause | Effect |
|---|---|
| *Adam*<br>• *Chose to follow Eve instead of God*<br>•<br>• | •<br>•<br>• |
| *Eve*<br>• *Chose to listen to serpent's lies instead of God's truth*<br>• | •<br>•<br>• |
| *Serpent*<br>•<br>•<br>• | •<br>•<br>• |

**Christian self-government**

3. Explain what *self-government* means to you.

4. Relate this principle to your life by listing ways you can improve your own Christian self-government.

# The Flood
## Genesis 6–9

**There is a beginning to time and everything that exists.**

After Creation and the Fall, the next event in the study of the beginnings is the Flood. After sin entered the world through the choices of Adam and Eve, evil continued to increase to the point that God was grieved that He had made man. Genesis chapter six describes what God saw, how He felt, and what He planned to do. Read Genesis chapter six to find out the details.

We learn several things about God in this chapter. One is that God is grieved by our sin and sin brings judgment from God. However, even though God judges sin, He also shows His mercy toward mankind and provides for restoration. We see this in His plan to preserve the righteous Noah, his family, and the animals so that the earth could be repopulated. Then God did an amazing thing: God promised Noah He would never destroy the earth again with a flood and gives him a sign of His promise. Read Genesis 9:11–17 to discover the sign.

### *Discussion and Notebook Work*

1. Use Webster's 1828 *Dictionary* and your Bible dictionary-concordance to record the definition for *covenant*. Read the related Scriptures.

2. Write your own definition based on your understanding of covenant.

3. Complete a **story map** of the Flood on a form from your teacher.

4. Use your **story map** information to write a paragraph summarizing what God saw, how He felt, and what He planned to do.

# The Tower of Babel
## Genesis 11

To review our study of the beginnings of Old Testament history, we have learned about three key events—the Creation, the Fall, and the Flood. After the Flood, the earth was repopulated through Noah's sons (Shem, Ham, and Japheth) and their wives as they had sons of their own. It was God's will for the people to spread out over the face of the earth. However, the result of the Fall remained in mankind: it was the sin of rebellion against God's will.

Study the fourth key event in the study of the beginnings by reading Genesis 11:1–9 to discover how the people rebelled against God at the tower of Babel. The tower was a monument for the people's pride rather than an honor to God. They sought a name for themselves, unity, and safety by building this great tower.

God is the Creator and Source of everything that exists.

It is thought by many Bible scholars that the tower of Babel was like a pyramid with a temple on top for the worship of false gods, perhaps the heavens. Today, the meaning of *Babel* stands for "confusion." We see here that God has power over creation—He changed the language of the people so they could no longer understand one another. This accomplished God's original plan, which was for the people to spread out over the earth, and punished the people for worshipping idols.

### Discussion and Notebook Work

1. Use the Webster's 1828 *Dictionary* and your Bible dictionary-concordance to record the definition for *unity*. Read the related Scriptures.

2. The unity of the people at the tower of Babel was in rebellion against God's will. Complete the **cause-and-effect organizer** to answer the questions:

   ⋆ What was the effect of the people's rebellion and desire for unity?
   ⋆ What was the effect of God's displeasure?

### The Consequences at the Tower of Babel

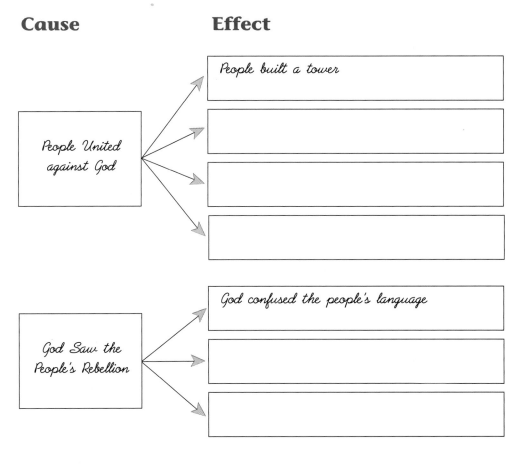

**Cause**      **Effect**

People United against God → People built a tower

God Saw the People's Rebellion → God confused the people's language

3. Reread Genesis 11:4 again and summarize what you learned about the character of the people.

# The Formation of a Nation through Abraham
## Genesis 12–13

Last week you read of some high points and low points in God's relationship with man and His enduring love and provision for mankind in spite of the sin of rebellion. The study this week begins a new chapter as God chooses a man and his descendents to carry out His plan for the world. The man's name is Abram and you will find the story of God calling Abram to follow Him in Genesis 12:1–8. Read this for yourself before proceeding with this lesson.

In the New Testament, Hebrews 11:8 says the following about Abram's call from God: "By faith Abraham, when called to go to a place he would later receive as his inheritance, obeyed and went, even though he did not know where he was going." (You may have noticed that Abram's name was changed, you'll learn about that later!) Think about what it took for Abram to leave his home. Without a doubt, it took faith! He was leaving his country and his relatives to go to a place he did not know. He sacrificed to follow and obey God by leaving all that was familiar and safe behind. It was a big decision for him. Abram was seventy-five years old at the time. He had to pack up the belongings of his family and the many people who accompanied him on a trip of about 1,500 miles to the land of Canaan. That's like walking halfway across the continent of North America!

Look back over the verses you read. Did you notice the promises God made to Abram? These promises were the beginning of the Hebrew nation that we know as Israel. Now complete the reading of chapter twelve and read chapter thirteen.

God created man for relationship with Him.

### Discussion and Notebook Work
1. Record the memory verse and file.

   "By faith Abraham, when called to go to a place he would later receive as his inheritance, obeyed and went, even though he did not know where he was going." (Hebrews 11:8)

2. Practice the verse to recite at the end of the week.

3. Use your Bible dictionary-concordance to record definitions for *descendant* and *inheritance*. Read the related Scripture references.

4. Begin a **sequence chain** of Abram's life as you study this week's lesson, The Formation of a Nation through Abraham. (See the model chart below.)

The Formation of a Nation through Abraham

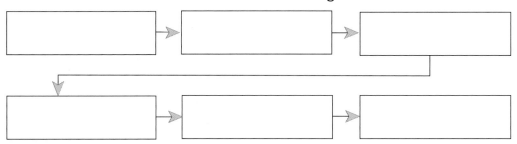

5. Ask your Mom and Dad to help you draw your family tree to discover your beginnings.

## God's Covenant with Abram
### Genesis 14–15

I would like to say that Abram obeyed God perfectly and was always a model of faith, but that was not true. In Genesis chapters twelve through thirteen, we read of some instances when Abram displayed little faith. You may have noticed that when we obey God, He blesses us and gives us more revelation of who He is and His plan for our lives. God did the same with Abram as he grew in faith and obedience. Be encouraged by this, because it gives us hope that we can grow in our faith and obedience like Abram. Take time to read Genesis chapter fourteen now to see how Abram grew in his walk of faith with God.

Do you remember the covenant God made with Noah? Well, God made a covenant with Abram as well that promised something different. God dem-

God created man for relationship with Him.

onstrated this covenant with a special ceremony that was familiar to the people of Abram's day. It was called a *covenant of blood*. Instead of two parties agreeing to the covenant, like our contracts today, God alone entered into covenant with Abram and promised the land of Canaan to Abram unconditionally. When God called Abram in Genesis chapter twelve, He made promises to him that were enlarged and confirmed in Genesis chapter fifteen in what is known as the *Abrahamic covenant*. As you read Genesis chapter fifteen, picture the ceremony of the blood covenant and the seriousness of it. This covenant is a picture of the future sacrifice of our Savior, Jesus Christ.

### Discussion and Notebook Work

1. Use your Bible dictionary-concordance to review and record the definition and understanding of *covenant*. Then read the related Scripture verses.

2. Read Genesis chapters fourteen and fifteen. Use the **SQ3R strategy** explained by the teacher to help you understand and remember the events in these chapters. Record your questions.

3. Add the events of Genesis chapters fourteen and fifteen to your **sequence chain.**

# Learning to Wait on God
## Genesis 16

Patriarch means the father of a family or tribe. The book of Genesis from chapter twelve through chapter fifty is an account of how God moved through the patriarchs (Abraham, Isaac, Jacob, and Joseph) to establish the nation of Israel. Stop for a moment and read Genesis 16. In this chapter you learn how Abram and Sarai fell into unbelief and tried to manipulate the circumstances themselves to make God's promise of children happen. Since Sarai was childless, she asked Abram to have a child with her maid, which was a common practice in that day. However, when Sarai's maid, Hagar, became pregnant, Hagar despised Sarai and Sarai mistreated Hagar. Therefore Hagar ran away into the desert where an angel of the Lord confronted her. Hagar was told to name the child *Ishmael* meaning "whom God hears" and to return to her mistress and to submit to Sarai. God promised Hagar many descendants and she obeyed His command.

The compromise of Abram and Sarai in trying to bring about God's promise has caused great strife over the centuries. Ishmael became the father of the Arab nations, who are the enemies of Israel to this day. Abram was 86 years old at the time and didn't hear God speak to him again for thirteen years—until he was 99 years old. At this time God changed Abram's name to Abraham. *Abram* means "exalted father," *Abraham* means "father of a multitude." God brought His promise to pass for Abraham and Sarah when Isaac was born.[1]

*God created man for relationship with Him.*

### Discussion and Notebook Work

1. Use Webster's 1828 *Dictionary* to complete a **vocabulary word analysis chart** for *compromise*.

2. Continue to add the events of this lesson to your **sequence chain**.

3. Does today's reading remind you of any time in your life when you tried to take things into your own hands when they should have been left up to God? Write a paragraph describing your experience and what you learned from it.

# Foreshadowing of a Savior
## Genesis 22

Have you ever used your hand to make shadows on the wall in the shape of an animal? What fun it is! The shadow is not the real thing, but it is a picture that reminds us of the real thing. A foreshadowing in Scripture is like this: it is a picture of something that is to come.

In the life of Abraham, there came a great trial that tested his faith in God and his willingness to obey Him at any cost to himself. God asked Abraham to sacrifice his only son, Isaac. Although this was a common practice among heathen nations at the time, God always hated human sacrifice. Read Genesis 22:1–18 to learn how Abraham's faith was tested.

*God created man for relationship with Him.*

### Discussion and Notebook Work

1. Use the Webster's 1828 *Dictionary* to record the definition for *foreshadowing*.

2. Record and answer the reason questions.

   a. What does the fact that Abraham rose early in the morning to do as God asked mean to you?

   b. In verse 5, Abraham told his servants to wait with the donkey while he and Isaac went to worship and then says, "We will come again to you." What does this say about Abraham's faith in God?

   c. When Isaac asked his father where the lamb for the burnt offering was, what was Abraham's reply?

   d. Abraham had already tied his son to the altar and taken the knife to kill him when God stopped him. Why did God allow him to go so far?

   e. Why did Abraham call the place, "The Lord Will Provide"?

   f. Abraham's offering of his only son, Isaac, foreshadows a New Testament event. Tell what event is being foreshadowed.

3. Continue to add events to your **sequence chain** for Abraham.

*Our relationship with God requires obedience.*

# The Judges of Israel
## Judges 2

God appoints leaders to govern His people.

The second link on the American Christian history timeline is Moses and the Law. The study of this link includes the Ten Commandments, the receiving of the Law, the history of Israel leaving Egypt, and the military conquest of Canaan led by Joshua. However, we are jumping over these events to the period of the judges. After Joshua died, the nation did not successfully drive out all the inhabitants of the land as the Lord had told them to do. The Canaanites became a snare to the Israelites and led them into the sin of idolatry. God then judged the nation of Israel and allowed them to be defeated by other nations or tribes. When Israel cried out to the Lord in repentance, God brought deliverance through individuals He raised up to lead Israel called *judges*. This was a cycle in the history of Israel that was repeated over and over again. We will study several of the judges such as Deborah, Gideon, and Samson. But first read Judges, chapter two to learn the history of Israel that brought about the need for judges.

### Discussion and Notebook Work

1. Read the memory verse and file.

   "In those days there was no king in Israel, but every man did that which was right in his own eyes." (Judges 17:6)

2. Practice the memory verse to recite at the end of the week.

3. Complete a **word map** for *idolatry*. See sample below.

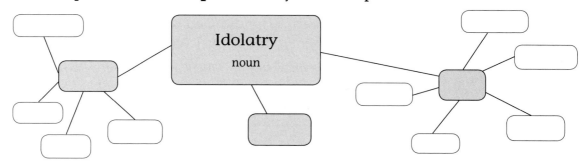

4. Use a **cyclical organizer** to demonstrate the cycle of sin, judgment, repentance, and deliverance found from reading the second chapter of Judges. List the events under each heading.

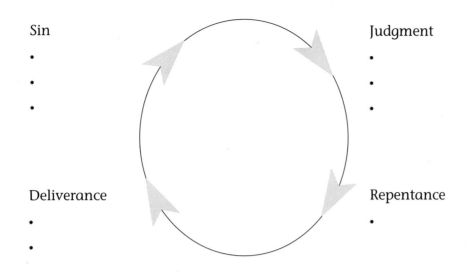

Sin
·
·
·

Judgment
·
·
·

Deliverance
·
·

Repentance
·

5. Read the special feature "Let's Live It: A Family History" and tell what God has done for your own family.

# The Importance of Leadership
## Judges

In your previous reading, you learned that Israel "groaned under those who oppressed and afflicted them," and God was merciful. He raised judges to authority whom He had given the skills to lead and to deliver Israel from their enemies. Some have said, "Mercy is not giving a person what he deserves." In the study of Judges, we will certainly see God's patience with Israel as they repeatedly turned away and sinned against Him.

God appoints leaders to govern His people.

### *Discussion and Notebook Work*
1. Complete a **word study** for *leader* using the Webster's 1828 *Dictionary*.
2. Skim the book of Judges in your Bible to locate and read the "People in Bible Times" feature for Deborah, Gideon, and Samson.

# Deborah
## Judges 4–5

In many cultures at the time of the judges and in many lands even today, women are not respected or allowed to lead. They hold only the lower positions of society. Even though women have a God-ordained role to fulfill in the family, God does not keep women from accomplishing great things. He chose Deborah and she was recognized in Israel as a prophetess and judge over the land.

You have completed a **word study** on *leader*. To learn about the leadership of Deborah, read Judges chapters four and five. Chapter five is a song of Deborah and Barak that tells of the victory over the enemies of Israel.

### Discussion and Notebook Work

1. Read the special feature "Let's Live It: Just for Girls" found in Judges four to learn about the leadership qualities of Deborah.

2. Write a sentence or two for each point of the leader acrostic below telling what you have learned about Deborah from your reading. Record the verse(s) where you found the information. (See the example provided below.)

**L**ives for God

**E**ncourages and enables others

**A**ttributes honor to God for success *She knew God was responsible for the victory ahead of time and communicated this to Barak. (v. 14)*

**D**elegates responsibility

**E**xperienced and confident

**R**espects self, respects others, and others respect her

3. Participate in a **Readers Theatre activity** using the song of Deborah in Judges chapter five.

# Gideon
## Judges 6–7

All through the Bible, we see God calling people just like you and me to do things that seem impossible. For instance, God placed Joseph in a position as a slave to be raised to a high place in Egypt so that his family might be saved. God called Moses, who was an outcast shepherd at the time, to lead Israel out of bondage in Egypt. Gideon was a farmer whom God called to be the fifth judge of Israel and to deliver Israel from their oppressors. Some of these men were fearful and felt totally unable to do what God asked of them.

Remember how Abraham was honored in Hebrews chapter eleven for his faith? Gideon is also described there as a man of faith. "And what shall I more say? I do not have time to tell about Gideon, Barak, Samson, Jephthah, David, Samuel, and the prophets, who through faith conquered kingdoms, administered justice, and gained what was promised; who shut the mouths of lions, quenched the fury of the flames, and escaped the edge of the sword; whose weakness was turned to strength; and who became powerful in battle and routed foreign armies." (Hebrews 11:32–34) The phrase "whose weakness was turned to strength," shows what God can do with a person who surrenders his life to Him like Gideon did.

During this period, the Midianites were oppressing Israel and would destroy their crops and animals so that the Israelites did not have enough food to eat or to sell. Gideon was threshing wheat in the winepress so the Midianites would not see the wheat and come to take it.

An angel of the Lord spoke to him saying, "The LORD is with you, mighty warrior." The Lord told Gideon that His hand was upon him to save Israel from the Midianites. Gideon was not sure God had the right person for the job. As if the Lord did not know of his circumstances, Gideon said, "My clan is the weakest in Manasseh, and I am the least in my family."

It took some convincing, but Gideon finally believed that God had been talking to him. He obeyed God's commands to tear down the altar to Baal in his father's house and cut down the trees beside it and made a burnt sacrifice to God there. (The trees were one of the ways people worshipped the idol Baal.) Gideon tore down the idol's altar at night with ten servants because

God appoints leaders to govern His people.

the idol-worshipping Israelites would kill him. This showed how much Israel wanted to serve other gods.

The next we hear, the Midianites came to attack Israel and "the Spirit of the LORD came upon Gideon." He began to gather troops from the various

tribes for battle, but then he doubted that God had really told him to lead Israel in battle against the Midianites. He asked for a sign from God that Israel would be saved by his hand. (Read about this test in Judges 6:37–40.) Today we have God's Word the Bible, the Holy Spirit in us, and prayer to teach us God's will for us. Even so, we may become afraid like Gideon and be tempted to doubt God's guidance.

After God confirmed His word to Gideon by doing as he had asked, Gideon prepared for battle. However, God now tested Gideon and his soldiers to see whether they truly trusted Him by reducing their numbers. Read Judges chapter seven to see how God delivered Israel through Gideon's leadership.

### Discussion and Notebook Work

1. Record and answer the reason questions.

   a. Why did God reduce the numbers of soldiers for the battle?

   b. How did God use the enemy soldier's dream to give Gideon courage to attack the Midianites?

2. Complete a **story map** using the information from the seventh chapter of Judges.

# Samson
## Judges 13

The following story of Samson was taken from *Golden Hours with the Bible*
by Catharine Shaw published by John F. Shaw & Co., Ltd.
This is an old book from the early 1900s with old-fashioned language.

After Joshua was dead, the Children of Israel began to be very slack in serving God; and worse than all, they set up other gods, and worshipped them, as the heathen did around them.

God was very long suffering, and He raised up judge after judge who delivered them from their enemies; but soon the people fell into idolatry again.

At length God was so grieved at their evil ways that He delivered them into the hands of the Philistines for twenty years. And then He raised them up another Judge.

There was a man who served God, whose name was Manoah; and he had a godly wife, but they had no children.

One day the Angel of the Lord appeared to Manoah's wife, and he told her that she would have the joy of having a little son, who, when he was grown, should deliver Israel from the hands of the Philistines.

But the angel gave Manoah's wife very strict instructions. Neither she, nor her child, were to take any wine or strong drink, and the boy was not to have a razor come on his head from the day of his birth to the day of his death! He was to be what was called, "A Nazarite unto God."

And Manoah prayed earnestly that God would send the angel to them again to tell them how to bring up the child who was to come to them.

And God listened to Manoah's prayer; and as the woman was in the field, the Angel came again to her; and she ran hastily to Manoah, and told him.

Then Manoah begged the man to let him dress a kid and offer him food—but the man said he would take no food, but they could offer a sacrifice to God, if they wished it.

And when the sacrifice was offered, and the smoke arose from the Altar, the Angel of the Lord went up toward heaven, and ascended in the flame from off the Altar.

Then Manoah said, "We shall surely die, because we have seen God!"

God appoints leaders to govern His people.

But his wife argued from all that had happened, that if the Lord had intended to kill them, He would not have accepted their offering, neither would He have showed them all these things.

At length the child came, and they called him Samson. As he grew to manhood, he found that God was giving him wonderful strength.[2]

### Discussion and Notebook Work

1. Record the memory verse and file.

   "He that is slow to anger is better than the mighty; and he that ruleth his spirit than he that taketh a city. (Proverbs 16:32)

2. Practice the memory verse for recitation at the end of the week.

3. Record the requirements to be a Nazarite?

4. Samson's parents committed to raising their son as a Nazarite. Today we dedicate children to God.

   ⋆ Use your Webster's 1828 *Dictionary* to record the definition of *dedicate*.
   ⋆ Complete a **concept/definition map** for *dedicate*.

5. Read the special feature "Let's Live It: Dedicating Children to the Lord." Ask your parents if you were dedicated or baptized as a baby and what promises were made. Record what you learn.

# Samson as a Young Man
## Judges 14

The following is a continuation of the story of Samson taken from
*Golden Hours with the Bible*
by Catharine Shaw published by John F. Shaw and Co., Ltd.

One day a young lion came out and roared against him. And the Spirit of the Lord came mightily upon him, and he rent the lion, and killed him, just as he might have rent a kid; for he had no weapon in his hand.

When Samson next passed that way, he looked for the carcass of the lion, and there it was lying by the path, and the bees were swarming around, as they had built a honeycomb in the body of the lion.

So he ate some of the honey, and took the rest to his father and mother; but he did not tell them that he had killed the lion.

Then Samson made a great feast for seven days, for he had married a Philistine girl, to the great sorrow of his parents; and while they were feasting, he and the thirty young men who were his companions, Samson gave them a riddle to find out, promising that he would give a large prize if they could discover it; but if not, they were to give him a prize.

This was the riddle: "Out of the eater came forth meat, and out of the strong came forth sweetness."

The young men puzzled for several days, and at last they persuaded Samson's young wife to get the secret from him; and at length she begged so hard that he told her the answer.

Then she went to her people, the Philistines, and told them.

When the seven days were up, the young men gave the answer: "What is sweeter than honey, and what is stronger than a lion?"

But Samson was very angry when he found that they had persuaded his wife; and he went down to Ashkelon and killed thirty Philistines, and brought the spoil and divided it among the young men who had answered his riddle; and then in fierce anger he returned to his father's house.

But his wife was given to one of the companions who used to be his friend, and Samson never saw her again.[3]

## Discussion and Notebook Work

1. Read Judges chapter fourteen to learn about Samson's marriage:
   * Why were his parents unhappy with his choice for a wife?
   * What did God think of his choice for a wife?
   * What did you learn about Samson's character from this story?
2. Record your answers.

# The Consequences of Revenge
## Judges 15

Read the definition of the noun *revenge* in the Webster's 1828 *Dictionary*. Read Judges chapter fifteen from your Bible and note the consequences of Samson taking revenge.

### *Discussion and Notebook Work*

1. Complete a **word wheel** on *revenge*.

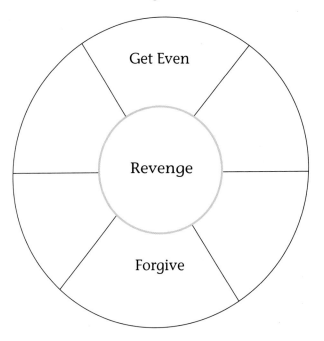

Get Even

Revenge

Forgive

2. Use the information from your reading and the **word wheel** to record how the cycle of revenge can be stopped.

3. Record and answer the reason questions.

   a. Do you think Samson was wise in taking revenge? Why or why not?

   b. Have you ever taken revenge on someone? Did you feel good or bad about the result? Explain.

4. In a paragraph, relate personal responses of what you should do when you are tempted to get even.

# The End of Samson's Life
## Judges 16

The following is a continuation of the story of Samson taken from
*Golden Hours with the Bible* by Catharine Shaw published by John F. Shaw and Co., Ltd.

Samson judged Israel for twenty years, and by his great personal strength and courage he gained many victories over the Philistines. But he made a great mistake, which resulted in his death. He again married a heathen Philistine woman.

The Philistines at once took advantage of this, and promised his wife great riches if she would find out, and tell them, the secret of his wonderful strength. In an evil moment he told her that it was because he was a Nazarite, and that no razor had ever come upon his head!

So, when he was asleep, Delilah managed to cut off his hair; and then she sent for the lords of the Philistines, who hurried to the spot. They easily bound Samson because his strength was gone from him; and they put out his eyes, and sent him to grind in the prison-house.

It would take me too long to tell you how his hair began to grow again, and his strength began to return, or how he was taken out to make sport for the Philistines, and how he begged the boy who led him to let him feel the pillars of the house where three thousand Philistines were watching him from the roof.

Samson asked God to give him strength for this, once more; and then he bowed himself with all his might, clasping the pillars in his arms, and the house fell, and he, and all the three thousand Philistines, were buried beneath the ruins.[4]

### Discussion and Notebook Work

1. Use a **K-W-L chart** to engage your thinking before, during, and after reading Judges chapter sixteen.

2. From the story of Samson's capture we learn that his great physical strength did not mean he had strong character. Which do you think is more important to develop in yourself, physical strength or strong character? Explain your answer.

3. Summarize and record the lessons you learned from the life of Samson.

# Samuel—God's Priest and Prophet
## 1 Samuel 1

From our study of the judges of Israel, it is clear that they were ordinary people—not perfect and often not very good leaders. However, the last judge over Israel was a Godly leader. His name was Samuel, which means "asked of God." His mother, Hannah, prayed to have a baby and then dedicated him to God before he was born. Remember, Samson's parents also dedicated him for God's service. However, the character of Samson and Samuel could not have been more different.

Have you ever wanted desperately for God to do something for you? What were you willing to do? The fact that Hannah wanted a child desperately can be seen in 1 Samuel chapter one. Read the chapter to find out what she did that indicated how badly she wanted a son.

### Discussion and Notebook Work

1. Record the memory verse and file.

   "Even a child is known by his doings, whether his work be pure, and whether it be right." (Proverbs 20:11)

2. Practice the memory verse to recite at the end of the week.

3. Complete a **sequence chain** for the birth and dedication of Samuel in 1 Samuel chapter one.

4. Use a **T-chart** to compare and contrast the character traits of Samson and Samuel. (See the special feature in your Bible, "People in Bible Times" or special tools found in other Bibles for additional information on Judges chapter thirteen and 1 Samuel chapter one.)

5. Record and answer the reason questions.

   a. Does God always answer our prayers?
   b. Does God always give us what we want?

6. Begin a prayer journal to record your prayer requests and how God answered them.

# Samuel's Call
## 1 Samuel 2–3

God appoints leaders to govern His people.

In 1 Samuel chapter one, you learned about the faith and character of Hannah, Samuel's mother, and how God answered her prayer for a son. She kept her vow (promise to God) by taking Samuel to live and serve in God's temple when he was very young. We know this from 1 Samuel 2:18–19, "But Samuel was ministering before the LORD—a boy wearing a linen ephod. Each year his mother made him a little robe and took it to him when she went up with her husband to offer the annual sacrifice." *Minister* means to attend and serve, or to give things needed. This shows us that even children can serve God. In 1 Samuel 2:26 we learn, "And the boy Samuel continued to grow in stature and in favor with the LORD and with men." You might be interested to know that Luke 2:52 says something similar about Jesus, "And Jesus grew in wisdom and stature, and in favor with God and men."

Learn how Samuel received his call from God by reading 1 Samuel chapter three. You will learn about the beginning of his training, which led to his becoming a priest, prophet, and judge over Israel.

The success of a leader depends on his obedience to God.

### *Discussion and Notebook Work*

1. Use your Webster's 1828 *Dictionary* and Bible dictionary-concordance to define *stature* and *favor*. Write a sentence using each word to demonstrate your understanding of the meaning.

2. Create a page similar to the one below and complete it with what you learned about Samuel's character from 1 Samuel chapter three.

3. Continue to add to your prayer journal.

### Samuel's Character

| Scripture | Conclusions about Samuel's Character |
|---|---|
| 1 Samuel 3:1<br>He ministered before the Lord under Eli. | *Samuel was obedient and humble.*<br>*Samuel was willing to be trained by Eli.* |
| 1 Samuel 3:5 "And he ran to Eli and said, 'Here I am; you called me.' " | |
| 1 Samuel 3:7a<br>"Now Samuel did not yet know the Lord." | |
| 1 Samuel 3:9<br>"Speak, Lord, for your servant is listening." | |
| 1 Samuel 3:15a<br>"Samuel lay down until morning and then opened the doors of the house of the Lord." | |
| 1 Samuel 3:18a "So Samuel told him everything, hiding nothing from him." | |
| 1 Samuel 3:19<br>"The Lord was with Samuel as he grew up, and he let none of his words fall to the ground." | |
| 1 Samuel 3:20 All Israel knew that Samuel was a prophet of the Lord. | |

# Samuel Anoints the First King of Israel
## 1 Samuel 8–10

Samuel was God's man and he led the nation under God's direction. This type of government is called a *theocracy*. Whenever their enemy, the Philistines, would rise up against Israel, the people would go to Samuel and ask him to pray to God to save them. Samuel told them to get rid of the false gods and only worship the Lord. When the people obeyed and Samuel prayed to the Lord, God had mercy on them and gave them victory over the enemy.

Eventually the people asked for a king to rule them like the nations around them, instead of being ruled by God through Samuel. This form of government is called a *monarchy*. This was a sad day for Samuel that is described in 1 Samuel chapter eight. God told Samuel, "It is not you they have rejected, but they have rejected me as their king." Samuel followed God's directions and told the people what it would be like for a king to rule over them. God then led Samuel to anoint Saul with oil as the first king of Israel. Read 1 Samuel 9–10:1 for an account of this momentous event in the history of the nation of Israel.

God appoints leaders to govern His people.

### Discussion and Notebook Work

1. Record the definitions for *theocracy* and *monarchy*.

2. Record and answer the reason questions.

   a. Why did the Israelites want a king?

   b. Explain why Saul was chosen as the first king of Israel.

   c. Relate a time when you were impressed by someone's outward appearance but later you changed your opinion because of their actions.

   d. What is the significance of anointing with oil? (See the special feature in your Bible, "Life in Bible Times: Anointing with Oil.")

3. Begin a **T-chart** on Saul's internal and external character qualities.

4. Continue to add to your prayer journal.

# Saul is Rejected by God
## 1 Samuel 13, 15

God appoints leaders to govern His people.

Saul was anointed king at the age of thirty and ruled for forty-two years. The new king started out with the Spirit of God upon him and did great things for Israel. However, little by little he turned from obeying God. One of his first mistakes was becoming impatient while waiting for Samuel to come and make an offering to the Lord before a big battle with the Philistines. Saul did not obey the Lord: he made the offering himself instead of waiting for Samuel, God's priest, to offer it. This shows the fear and unbelief in God's promises that was affecting Saul's decision making. Samuel told him that his kingdom would not last as the result of his disobedience to God. For the history of why Saul was rejected by God as Israel's king, read of this is found in 1 Samuel chapter thirteen.

The success of a leader depends on his obedience to God.

In 1 Samuel chapter fifteen, you can read how much Saul rebelled against God and how many sad changes he had made to his character. Read the reason questions below first and then read the Scriptures to answer the questions.

### Discussion and Notebook Work

1. Summarize briefly in your own words God's instructions to Saul about the battle with the Amalekites.

2. Record and answer the reason questions.

    a. How did Saul disobey God?

    b. What excuses did Saul make for his disobedience?

    c. Was Saul repentant? Explain.

    d. How did Samuel feel about Saul's sin?

3. Add to the **T-chart** describing Saul's internal and external character.

4. Use the information from the **T-chart** to explain why God rejected Saul as king of Israel.

5. Continue to add to your prayer journal.

# Samuel Anoints a New King
## 1 Samuel 16

Samuel was very grieved over the failure of Saul and God had to gently rebuke him for it. God had another man in mind to be king who was "a man after His own heart." He sent Samuel to anoint the new king from the family of a man named Jesse in Bethlehem.

Read 1 Samuel chapter sixteen to learn of one of the individuals most beloved by students of Old Testament history. This is the story of Samuel anointing David as the new king of Israel and how David first met Saul.

### Discussion and Notebook Work

1. Record the memory verse and file.

   "But the LORD said unto Samuel, Look not on his countenance, or on the height of his stature; because I have refused him: for the LORD seeth not as man seeth; for man looketh on the outward appearance, but the LORD looketh on the heart." (1 Samuel 16:7)

2. Practice the memory verse to recite at the end of the week.

3. Use your Bible dictionary-concordance:

   ★ To define *heart*.
   ★ To read the related Scriptures to understand what the Bible says about the heart.
   ★ To answer the question: When God looks at your heart what does He see?

4. Read Proverbs 4:23 to understand why God wants us to guard our hearts. Explain what this means to you.

5. Begin a **T-chart** on your paper and identify the internal and external character qualities of David from your reading this week.

   David's Character Qualities
   | Internal | External |
   | --- | --- |

6. Continue to add to your prayer journal.

# The Testing of David
## 1 Samuel 17–19, 24

God looks
on the heart
of a man to
determine
his character.

I'm sure you have heard the story of David and Goliath many times. David was a teenager when the Philistine army came to fight Israel. David had traveled to the battlefront to bring food for his brothers. He heard the taunts of Goliath against the army of Israel and said, "Who is this uncircumcised Philistine that he should defy the armies of the living God?" You can see by this statement that even as a youth he had a reverence and fear of the Lord. He was God's chosen one to defeat Goliath.

Even though he had been anointed to be king, many years went by before this actually came to pass. In the mean time David endured many trials that refined him and made him into "a man after God's own heart." The following describes one of those trials.

The following story about David is taken from
*Golden Hours with the Bible* by Catharine Shaw
published by John F. Shaw & Co., Ltd.

After David had conquered the giant, and had brought is head to the King, Saul for a while was very proud of his young soldier, and made much of him in every way; and David behaved himself wisely; and Saul set him over his men of war, and he became very popular among the people.

Meanwhile Jonathan, Saul's son, thought there was no one in the world like David! He loved him as his own soul.

He took off his own beautiful clothes, which belonged to him as the king's son, and put them on David, even presenting him with his sword, his bow and his girdle.

But a jealous feeling began to rankle in the breast of the king.

He heard the women singing who came out to meet him from the cities, after David's slaughter of the giant, and these were the words they sang: "Saul has slain his thousands, but David his ten thousands."

This made the king very angry, and from that day forth he determined to kill David.

60         Old Testament History

So King Saul hunted David up and down the land. Jonathan was devoted to him, and helped him to escape many times. He endeavored to be a peacemaker, and assured his father that David had no evil designs against him. But it was all of no use. Jealousy, which the Bible says is "cruel as the grave," had entered into Saul's heart, and it poisoned all his thoughts.

Then David again had a great victory over the Philistines, and Saul was so jealous that he threw his javelin at him. David, however, escaped, and the javelin went into the wall, where he had been sitting playing his harp to Saul.

He fled to his house, but Saul sent men to watch for him and to kill him in the morning. So Michal, his wife, persuaded him to fly that night, for she was sure he would be slain.

Michal was Saul's daughter, and she loved David. So she let him down through a window, and he escaped.

Then Michal took an image, and laid it in the bed, and put a goat's-hair pillow for a bolster and covered it with a cloth.

And when Saul's messengers came to take David, Michal said: "He is sick."

Then Saul sent back the messengers and ordered them to bring David in his bed!

But when the messengers came in there was only an image in the bed, and David was far away!

So it went on, till David was hunted from place to place, all over the land, and driven, with the men of war who followed him, to live in the mountains, and among rocks and caves, to get away from Saul's vengeance.

One day as Saul was pursuing hotly after David, who he heard was in the wilderness of Engedi, he was very weary with travel, and finding a large dark cave, he entered it, and lay down to get some sleep.

Little did Saul guess that the man he had come to seek was close to him, and that in the darkness of the cave, and hidden by the jutting sides, David and his men were quietly watching him.

When Saul had fallen into a deep sleep, David's men whispered to him that the day had come when the Lord had delivered his enemy into his hand!

So David went forward, and as he approached Saul he saw that his robe, with which he had covered his feet, lay partly on the ground. So he softly cut off the skirt of Saul's robe, and went back to his hiding-place.

But David's heart smote him, because he had cut off Saul's robe; and he hastily forbade his men to touch the king, for was he not the Lord's anointed?

Presently Saul awoke from his sleep and went out of the cave, and David followed him and called out to him, "My lord the king!" And when Saul looked behind him, David stooped and bowed low before him.

And David said to Saul: "Why do you regard men's words, telling you that I seek your hurt? Look, how this very day the Lord has delivered you into my hand in the cave, and some bade me kill you; but my eye has spared you, and I said, 'I will not put forth my hand to hurt the Lord's anointed!' Moreover, see, my father, here is the skirt of your robe in my hand! Surely you know now that I have not tried to hurt you, and yet you have hunted my soul to take it! The Lord is judge between us: He will plead my cause, and will deliver me out of your hand!"

When David had said these gentle and brave words, Saul said: "Is this thy voice, my son David?" and Saul lifted up his voice and wept.

Then he said to David: "You have been more honourable than I have, for you have rewarded me with good, and I have rewarded you with evil. Therefore may the Lord reward you good for what you have done to me this day."

And then he went on to tell David that he knew he would be king one day, and he earnestly begged him to be merciful to his father's house and not let his name perish out of the land.

So David promised him, before the Lord.

Then Saul went to his house, and David returned to his stronghold.[5]

### *Discussion and Notebook Work*

1. Pair off and share your thinking with a partner to answer the questions from the story of David.

   ★ Why was David unafraid of Goliath?
   ★ Why was Saul jealous of David?
   ★ How did Jonathan demonstrate his love and friendship to David?
   ★ How did Michal demonstrate her faithfulness?
   ★ How was David tested?
   ★ What was David's response to the testing?

2. Use your Bible dictionary-concordance to record the definitions of *jealous* and *jealousy*.

   a. Read the related Scripture verses.
   b. Write sentences to demonstrate the different meanings for *jealous* and *jealousy*.

3. Continue to add David's character qualities to the **T-chart**.

4. Continue to add to your prayer journal.

# Trials Reveal Character
## 1 Samuel 26, 31; and 2 Samuel 1

We have seen David as a shepherd, poet, musician, and soldier. His character is further revealed as God prepares him to be king and after becoming king; some of what we learn is good and some is bad.

Even though David had spared Saul in the cave and had been shown to be honorable and loyal to the king, Saul once again tried to find David to kill him! As Saul and his army camped in the wilderness, David and a couple of his men went down to the camp while the army was sleeping. One of his men wanted David to kill Saul, but David refused saying, "Don't destroy him! Who can lay a hand on the LORD's anointed and be guiltless?" (1 Samuel 26:9) Instead David took Saul's spear and water jug near his head and left.

David left Saul's camp and called out to the army asking of Saul, "Why is my lord pursuing his servant? What have I done, and what wrong am I guilty of?" David said that he meant Saul no harm and that the proof was Saul's missing spear and water jug. When Saul saw the truth of David's words, he repented and stopped trying to kill David.

Then David returned Saul's spear and said, "The LORD rewards every man for his righteousness

> God looks on the heart of a man to determine his character.

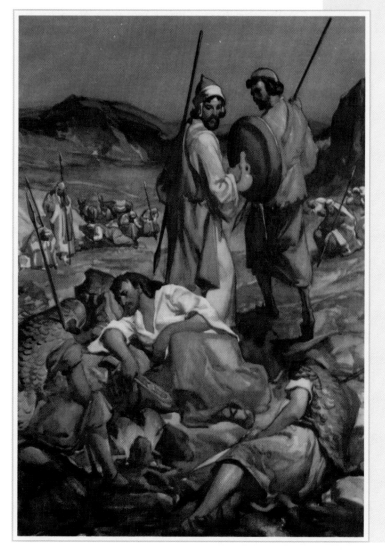

and faithfulness. The LORD delivered you into my hands today, but I would not lay a hand on the LORD's anointed. As surely as I valued your life today, so may the LORD value my life and deliver me from all trouble." (1 Samuel 26:23–24)

All David's troubles didn't go away, but God was faithful to deliver him out of the troubles that came his way.

The next thing David heard about Saul is his death in battle. David is truly saddened by the news and the Bible says that he and "all the men with him took hold of their clothes and tore them. They mourned and wept and fasted till evening for Saul and his son Jonathan, and for the army of the LORD and for the house of Israel, because they had fallen by the sword." (2 Samuel 1:11–12)

To express his sorrow for the loss of Saul and Jonathan, David wrote a lament. A *lament* is a song used to express a person's sorrow. Read the lament for Saul and Jonathan written by David in 2 Samuel 1:17–27. Have you ever seen someone so pure in heart as David and quick to forgive? He gave honor to someone in authority over him whose behavior did not merit honor. This is Godly conduct. Scripture says to give honor to whom honor is due. It doesn't say to give honor if the person in authority over you deserves it.

### Discussion and Notebook Work

1. Use your Webster's 1828 *Dictionary* to record the definitions for *lament* as a noun and as a verb.

2. Write sentences using *lament* as a noun and as a verb.

3. Continue to add to the **T-chart** of David's character qualities.

4. Participate in a **Readers Theatre activity** using David's lament for Saul and Jonathan in 2 Samuel 1:17–27. Read and perform for your classmates using your best oral reading skills.

5. Continue to add to your prayer journal.

# The Fallen Nature of a Great King
## 2 Samuel 11–12; Psalm 51

There were many other instances when David's Godly character was revealed. Lest you think David was perfect, you need to know that he also was a man who sinned—yet he repented and accepted the consequences of his sins.

Dear one, know that our sins are always found out. There is nothing hidden from God. David sinned with another man's wife and then had her husband sent to the front lines of a battle where he was sure to be killed. David's sin was revealed by God to the prophet Nathan, and he confronted David. The baby that resulted from this sin died even after David repented and pleaded with God to heal the child. The consequences of our sin can have lasting affects not only for us, but others as well.

Read David's story of sin, repentance, and forgiveness in 2 Samuel chapters eleven through twelve. Also read Psalm chapter fifty-one to see David's heart of repentance.

God looks on the heart of a man to determine his character.

1. Use your Bible dictionary-concordance to record the definitions for *iniquity, repentance,* and *forgiveness.*
2. Use a timeline to record the series of events in 2 Samuel chapters eleven through twelve about the sin of David. (Highlight his sin, his repentance, and his forgiveness.)
3. Use cause-and-effect reasoning from the timeline to summarize and record the consequences of David's actions.
4. Complete the **T-chart** of David's character qualities.
5. In Psalm chapter fifty-one, David recognized his sin was against God. In your prayer time, ask God to forgive your sins. Then pray Psalm 51:10.
6. Continue to add to your prayer journal.

# The History of the Temple
### 2 Samuel 7; 1 Kings 5–7; 1 Chronicles 28:3

God
wants a
relationship
with us.

In our study of Old Testament history thus far, you have seen how important their relationship with God was to the people of Israel. God had given Moses the plan for the Tabernacle as a visible representation of God's presence among the people. It was carried from place to place as the people moved through the wilderness and during the conquering of Canaan. The instructions God gave Moses for the Tabernacle are found in Exodus chapters twenty-five through thirty. Read the definition for *tabernacle* in your Bible dictionary-concordance to find the other name for *tabernacle.*

Earlier, you learned that God had providentially planned certain events in the history of the nation of Israel to foreshadow things to come. Read the Webster's 1828 *Dictionary* definition for *tabernacle* and you will find reference to the tabernacle of God in the New Testament.

After God helped the Israelites conquer Canaan and the people were established in houses, David became king. Now, David had it in his heart to build a permanent house or *temple* for God, but God would not allow David to build it because he was a man of war (1 Kings 5:3 and 1 Chronicles 22:7–8). He promised that David's son would build the temple. However, God did give David the plans for the temple, and allowed him to collect many of the materials for it, which were later used by his son Solomon. Read 2 Samuel chapter seven to find out God's promises to David.

After Solomon became king, he carried out the plans of his father. The temple built by Solomon had the same general structure as the Tabernacle of Moses, but it was permanent and twice as big. Read the definition for *temple* in the Webster's 1828 *Dictionary* and in your Bible dictionary-concordance.

### Discussion and Notebook Work

1. Record the memory verse and file.

   "And what agreement hath the temple of God with idols? for ye are the temple of the living God; as God hath said, I will dwell in them, and walk in them; and I will be their God, and they shall be my people." (2 Corinthians 6:16)

2. Practice the memory verse to recite at the end of the week.

3. Record the definitions for *tabernacle* and *temple*.

4. Read 2 Corinthians 5:1, 6:16; 2 Peter 1:13–14, and Ephesians 2:19–22 for information on the tabernacle/temple. In a paragraph explain what the New Testament house for God was and where it is located.

5. Relate how you make a plan to carry out a big job. (Hints: cleaning your room, completing a school project, helping a neighbor, planning an event)

6. Continue to add to your prayer journal.

# The Orchestration of a Mighty Big Building Project
## 2 Chronicles 1–2; 1 Kings 6–7

The Lord knows what He is doing when He chooses someone to do a job. Solomon had a dream where he asked God for wisdom and knowledge to lead the people of Israel. God agreed and also promised to give him great wealth and honor and a long life. You can see Solomon's wisdom and knowledge in his management while building the Temple. Since the Temple would be the center of worship in Jerusalem and the place where the yearly holy feasts were celebrated, Solomon wanted God's Temple to be a place of beauty and magnificence that would honor the God of the universe.

To accomplish this great task, Solomon called for the best and most skilled workers—some of them weren't even from Israel! God gives gifts and talents to all men whether they know Him or not. Solomon coordinated the work and made an agreement with another king to get the supplies and laborers he needed to build God the very best temple he could.

Read the account of the preparations for building the Temple in 2 Chronicles chapter two. Look to see how Solomon speaks about God to this foreign king, King Hiram of Tyre.

### Discussion and Notebook Work

1. Begin to complete a **"People Who Impacted History" chart** on Solomon and record what you learned.

2. Relate what you would do if God appeared to you as He did to Solomon in 2 Chronicles 1:7.

3. Continue to add to your prayer journal.

*Enrichment activity*—Read 1 Kings 6 and 7:13–51 to find a description of the building of the Temple.

# The Completion of the Temple
## 2 Chronicles 4–5

An earlier lesson mentioned that the Temple was a permanent building instead of a portable tent like the tabernacle. The layout and furnishings of the Temple were patterned after the tabernacle because they had special meaning. Each of these structures is a picture (shadow, type) of Jesus and His sacrifice for us so we could be forgiven of our sins and have fellowship with God.

Read 2 Chronicles 4:19–22 and chapter five and look at the pictures your teacher has brought for you. As you read, see if you can locate the places in the Temple and the items being described.

The ark of the Lord's covenant containing the ten commandments that God gave Moses and the Israelites was placed in the Most Holy Place. A curtain with blue, purple, and crimson threads and fine linen with cherubim sewn in it separated the Most Holy Place from the Holy Place. In the Holy Place were ten golden tables for the bread of the Presence or *showbread*, ten golden lampstands, and an altar of incense. Outside the Holy Place in the Temple court was a laver also called the "molten sea." It was used by the priests for washing before performing their priestly duties and to fill ten smaller lavers for washing the animal sacrifices. The laver was near the altar where the animal sacrifices were burned.

There is special meaning for us in all God's instructions to us, and the construction of the Temple and its furnishings are no different.

The altar for offering animal sacrifices reminded the people that the animal had been put to death for their sins. They believed God that Messiah would one day come to pay the price for their sins. This was a shadow of Jesus who went to the cross and died for our sins once and for all making the repeated offering of animals unnecessary.

The laver was made of bronze, which represented the judgment of sin. The priests were to wash their hands and feet in the water of the laver before entering the Temple to keep them from dying. This represents the cleansing of our sins through Jesus. Jesus is the Word and we are cleansed by the washing of the Word. (See Ephesians 5:26; 1 John 1:9; Psalms 119:9; and John 15:3.)

God wants a relationship with us.

God chose the children of Israel to be His people and gave them instructions for a Temple.

The table of showbread in the Holy Place could only be eaten by the priests. This represents to us the Bread of Life, who is Jesus. We receive the Bread of Life (eternal life) only by receiving Jesus and having our sins washed away by His sacrifice and the shedding of His blood on the cross for us.

The lampstand with oil in the seven bowls in the Holy Place was never to go out but always be kept burning by the priests. It represents the light that God's people receive. This light is to be a testimony to the world so others may come to know the Savior who is the Light of the world.

On the altar of incense, priests were to burn the holy anointing oil and sweet incense continually. This represents to us the sweet fragrance that prayer is to God. Only those who have been cleansed of their sin can come to God in prayer by faith.

The Ark of the Covenant was in the Most Holy Place and was covered with the mercy seat. The high priest went in once a year and sprinkled the blood of the sacrifice on it for the remission of sin. This represents the fact that God has judged our sin because of the blood of Jesus Christ. We receive mercy and grace and the forgiveness of our sins. Therefore, nothing separates us from God and we can fellowship with Him.

### *Discussion and Notebook Work*

1. Discuss and record how the Temple was a foreshadowing of the sacrifice of Jesus.

2. Record the furnishings of Solomon's Temple and what they represent.

3. Label and color a picture of Solomon's Temple.

4. Continue working on your **"People Who Impacted History" chart.**

5. Continue to add to your prayer journal.

# Solomon's Prayer of Dedication
## 1 Kings 5–8; 2 Chronicles 3–4

Our response to God's love is to worship Him in spirit and truth.

When studying the life of Samson, you learned the definition of *dedicate*. You may not realize this, but not only people can be dedicated (to set apart or consecrate to a divine Being, or to a sacred purpose), but buildings and material things can also be dedicated to God.

Solomon dedicated the Temple with a special prayer before the people of Israel. He reminded them that God keeps His covenant promises with people who continue in relationship with Him and follow His ways. Solomon acknowledged that no temple or even the heavens can contain God. He called on God to respond in mercy and forgiveness and hear their prayers when His people called upon Him in the Temple or toward it.

Solomon's prayer is an example for us of some things we can ask for in prayer and expect God to hear and answer if we are in right standing with Him. Read 1 Kings 8:31–45.

### Discussion and Notebook Work

1. In 1 Kings 8:31–45 are six examples of situations where prayer to God will bring about positive results. Use Solomon's prayer as a model to write your own prayer for a current day situation. (See the example provided below.)

   1 Kings 8:31–32—when a man wrongs his neighbor

   *Lord, I was falsely accused in class. Please reveal the truth to my teacher.*

   1 Kings 8:33–34—when God's people are defeated by an enemy

   1 Kings 8:35–36—when there is no rain

   1 Kings 8:37–40—when there is famine or plague

   1 Kings 8:41–43—when the foreigner prays to God

   1 Kings 8:44–45—when your people go to war defeat their enemies

2. Continue to add to the **"People Who Impacted History" chart.**

3. Continue to add to your prayer journal.

*Enrichment activity*—Read other passages about Solomon's Temple found in 2 Chronicles chapters two through four and 1 Kings chapters five through eight.

# The Fall of the Kingdoms of Israel and Judah
## 1 Kings 11–12, 14

**People suffer for sinful behavior.**

We have studied a time of tremendous blessing upon the nation of Israel, but now we come to a tremendous low. Old Testament history records how Solomon opened the door to the worship of foreign gods by marrying the daughters of foreign kings for political purposes. Because of his compromise, God allowed the kingdom to be divided after Solomon's death. Ten of the twelve tribes became the nation of Israel, which was also known as the Northern Kingdom. The other two tribes became the nation of Judah, or the Southern Kingdom.

Jesus said in the New Testament, "Every kingdom divided against itself will be ruined, and every city or household divided against itself will not stand."

Period of the Divided Kingdom

Northern Kingdom—Israel
Southern Kingdom—Judah

(Matthew 12:25) First and Second Kings tell the history of the two nations and how each one fell away from serving God. Time and time again the words are repeated for one nation or the other, "Judah did evil in the eyes of the LORD. By the sins they committed, they stirred up his jealous anger more than their fathers had done. They also set up for themselves high places, sacred stones and Asherah poles on every high hill and under every spreading tree." (1 Kings 14:22–23) There was the occasional good king, but mostly the kings of both nations led the people into sin. Again and again, the rule of the king was described by this statement, "He did evil in the eyes of the LORD."

In spite of the various prophets who ministered the word of the Lord to turn the people back to God, the people refused to repent. God is patient with man, but eventually judgment will come. There are consequences for sin. God allowed Israel and Judah to come under the judgment of foreign nations for four hundred ninety years. The nations through which judgment came were Assyria, Babylon, and Persia.

### Discussion and Notebook Work

1. Record the memory verse and file.

   "If my people, which are called by my name, shall humble themselves, and pray, and seek my face, and turn from their wicked ways; then will I hear from heaven, and will forgive their sin, and will heal their land." (2 Chronicles 7:14)

2. Practice the memory verse to recite at the end of the week.

3. Read 1 Kings 12:15 and 11:29–33.

   ★ Record what you learned about the split of the nation.
   ★ Record what you learned about God from your reading.

4. Complete the **"People Who Impacted History" chart** on Solomon.

5. Continue to add to your prayer journal.

# Captivity and Exile
## 2 Kings 25; 2 Chronicles 36; Psalm 137

The Babylonians invaded Judah twice. Each time the Babylonians took away the leaders—the educated, the skilled, and the strong people—to Babylon where they made new lives for themselves. Some, like Daniel, served in the king's palace. Others were educated in the ways of the land and used their talents to benefit the Babylonians.

The Babylonians destroyed the walls surrounding Jerusalem and burned down the Temple. They left the poor and weak alone in the land. Some were elevated to positions of leadership under the authority of the Babylonians.

Psalm 137:1–6 describes the sorrow of the captives. See if you can understand their pain. "By the rivers of Babylon we sat and wept when we remembered Zion. There on the poplars we hung our harps, for there our

People suffer for sinful behavior.

captors asked us for songs, our tormentors demanded songs of joy; they said, 'Sing us one of the songs of Zion!' How can we sing the songs of the LORD while in a foreign land? If I forget you, O Jerusalem, may my right hand forget its skill. May my tongue cling to the roof of my mouth if I do not remember you, if I do not consider Jerusalem my highest joy."

### *Discussion and Notebook Work*

1. Read 2 Chronicles chapter thirty-six to learn more about the rulers and about the destruction of the Temple.

   * Choose one king and write a brief summary telling what you learned about his reign.
   * Write a brief summary of what you learned about the destruction of the Temple.

2. Participate in the **Readers Theatre activity** for Psalm chapter one hundred thirty-seven.

# A Mission from God
## Ezra 1–7

People suffer for sinful behavior.

In the last lesson, you learned that God spoke to Cyrus, king of Persia, and told him to build Him a house in Jerusalem, which is in Judah. The book of Ezra is the history of some the people who returned to Jerusalem to begin rebuilding the Temple.

The Jews had been in captivity in Babylon for seventy years before the Persian Empire conquered Babylon. By that time, many of the exiled Jews had become wealthy and did not want to return to their homeland and start over. However, 50,000 people chose to make the journey and began the work of rebuilding the altar to reinstitute worship to the God of Israel. Upon completing the altar, offerings were made and all the feast days were once again celebrated.

In the second year of their return, rebuilding of the Temple was begun. But there were enemies who opposed the work and tried first to hinder and finally to stop the work any way they could. At first these enemies pretended to be worshippers of God and wanted to help with the building. When their help was refused, they then set about to discourage the people and make them afraid to continue the building. Then they hired counselors to frustrate the work. They wrote a letter to the faraway king saying the Jews would do many rebellious things if the work was allowed to be completed. The king had the work stopped for nearly a decade. The work eventually resumed and was completed.

This is where Ezra comes into the picture. He was a priest, scribe, teacher, and leader. He

was born in Babylon. His name means "help" and he certainly was a help to his people. He was appointed by the Persian emperor, Artaxerxes, to administrate the worship in the Temple, maintain justice for the people, and teach the laws of God that had been forgotten for so many years. God's hand was certainly upon him and God had providentially prepared the king to support him in God's call upon Ezra's life. Read the letter of King Artaxerxes to Ezra and his response in Ezra 7:11–28.

### Discussion and Notebook Work

1. Look in the Bible dictionary-concordance to review the definition of *favor*. From your reading, identify and record several ways that you see that Ezra had favor with the king.

2. Write Ezra's response to the king using the style from the letter in Ezra chapter four.

3. Record what you learned about God from this lesson.

4. Continue to add to your prayer journal.

# The Heart and Hands of a Leader
## Nehemiah 1–5

People suffer for sinful behavior.

Nehemiah was the cupbearer to King Artaxerxes, which means that he tasted the king's food to be sure it was not poisoned. It appears that he also was a trusted advisor and faithful servant. His ministry in Jerusalem began about thirteen years after Ezra had returned to Jerusalem.

We learn in the first chapter of Nehemiah how upset Nehemiah was when he learned of the trouble of the Jews who had returned to Jerusalem. They were exposed to their enemies because the walls of the city had not been repaired and therefore could not protect themselves. When Nehemiah heard of this, he immediately began to weep, mourn, fast, and pray. His prayer consisted of praise to God, confession of the sins of the nation, and petition to God reminding Him of promises of mercy if the people repented and prayed.

The king noticed Nehemiah's sadness and asked the reason for it. Nehemiah prayerfully and respectfully explained his concerns and asked for permission to return to Jerusalem to rebuild the walls. Just like Ezra, Nehemiah found favor with the king and was provided with the appropriate letters necessary to travel and to acquire the materials needed. He was also given protection by the king's army for the trip.

Upon returning to Jerusalem, the first thing Nehemiah did was go to see the walls for himself. Then he called the leaders of the city together to explain his calling. He inspired them with the vision, telling them that God's hand was upon them, and that they needed to proceed with faith instead of fear. He won their support by identifying with the people in their distress and confidently presenting his plan to help.

Nehemiah was a skilled administrator. He unified the people and organized them to work in different areas of the wall. He set some to work on the walls while others stood guard to protect the workers. He recorded the names of the workers, giving them credit for their labor. He steadfastly oversaw the work, solving problems, supporting, encouraging, helping, and dealing with the enemy when necessary. When opposition came, Nehemiah boldly confronted it with faith and prayer. Nehemiah is an example of a wise and good leader.

### Discussion and Notebook Work

1. Read Nehemiah 5:14–19 to identify and record at least four things that made Nehemiah a good leader.

2. Record and answer the reason questions.
   a. What did you learn about God in this lesson?
   b. How did God use Nehemiah to rebuild the walls of Jerusalem?

3. Read Nehemiah 4:1–23 to identify and record the challenges Nehemiah faced to rebuilding the wall and his responses to them.

4. Relate and record how God could use you right now to bless and protect His children.

5. Continue to add to your prayer journal.

# The Geography of the Ancient Middle East

God designed the geography of the earth to instruct man and to reveal His glory.

Modern geographers often refer to an area of land in the Middle East as the "Fertile Crescent." From a map it looks like a horseshoe stretching from the Persian Gulf northward along the Euphrates and Tigris Rivers. From the upper Euphrates, the fertile lowlands curve westward and descend to the Jordan River Valley and on south to the regions of the Nile River. Barriers of desert, mountains, and the sea made other routes impractical. Therefore, this route was heavily traveled by caravans of traders, shepherds looking for pasture for flocks, and people looking for food.

This highway connected Egypt and Babylon and often brought armies of invaders to conquer the peoples who lived along this highway. Consequently the lands between the Mediterranean Sea and the Persian Gulf were constantly changing hands throughout ancient history. The nations that conquered Israel during this time were the Assyrian Empire, the Babylonian Empire, and the Persian Empire.

The Persian Empire covered the greatest amount of land and lasted for two hundred years. It came to an end when Alexander the Great of Greece conquered the Persian Empire in 330 B.C. The Persian Empire was the one in control at the time of Ezra and Nehemiah.

Looking back on the history of this area and the location of Israel, one might reason that God placed Israel in this "cradle of civilization" in order to impact the world for Him.

Review *The Noah Plan*® Map Standard before beginning the map of the Ancient Middle East.

### Discussion and Notebook Work

1. Record the memory verse and file.

   "And hath made of one blood all nations of men for to dwell on all the face of the earth, and hath determined the times before appointed, and the bounds of their habitation." (Acts 17:26)

2. Practice the memory verse for recitation at the end of the week.

3. Label the following on your map according to the map standard.

| a. Waters: | b. Cities: | c. Nations: |
|---|---|---|
| The Mediterranean Sea | Jerusalem | Israel and Judah |
| The Tigris River | Damascus | Egypt |
| The Euphrates River | Babylon | |
| The Persian Gulf | Nineveh | |
| The Red Sea | Haran | |

4. Use different colored pencils to outline the regions covered by the different empires:

Assyrian Empire
Babylonian Empire
Persian Empire

[1] Information drawn from: Dr. H. L. Willmington, *Willmington's Guide to the Bible*. Wheaton: Tyndale House, 1987, 40.

[2] Catharine Shaw, *Golden Hours with the Bible*. John F. Shaw & Co., Ltd., 15.

[3] Ibid, 17.

[4] Ibid, 19.

[5] Ibid, 28.

[6] Rev. Paul C. Jong, *Tabernacle Study*. The New Life Mission Web site, http://www.bjnewlife.org/english/bstudy/tabernacle_study_10.

# Wisdom Literature and Prophecy

# Introduction to Wisdom Literature
## Job 28; Psalm 91; Proverbs 9; Isaiah 40;
## Romans 11; James 1; 2 Peter 1

Wisdom
comes
from God.

Job, Psalms, Proverbs, Ecclesiastes, and the Song of Solomon are books of the Bible that are classified to as wisdom literature. These are also the books of poetry. *Wisdom* is defined in the Dickson New Analytical Study Bible as, "The ability to judge fairly and to understand and make wise use of facts. The Hebrew conception was that wisdom is an attribute of God and that He shared it with certain men." According to Webster's 1828 *Dictionary* an *attribute* is a quality or characteristic, something belonging to an individual. We can gain wisdom by studying God's Word and by asking Him for it. James 1:5 in your Bible says, "If any of you lacks wisdom, he should ask God, who gives generously to all without finding fault, and it will be given to him."

Read the introductory pages of each book of the wisdom literature to get an overview of the purpose of each book.

### Discussion and Notebook Work

1. Record the memory verses and file.

   "He that dwelleth in the secret place of the Most High shall abide under the shadow of the Almighty. I will say of the LORD, He is my refuge and my fortress: my God; in him will I trust." (Psalm 91:1–2)

2. Practice the memory verses to recite later in the week.

3. Complete a **concept/definition map** for *wisdom*.

4. Read the following Scriptures to discover the Hebrew view of wisdom: Job 28:28, Isaiah 40:12–14, and Romans 11:33–35. Summarize and record what you learn.

5. Record and relate Proverbs 9:10 to the study of the Bible.

6. Read James 1:5 and 2 Peter 1:2–4 and describe what it means to be wise. Record your information.

# The Book of Psalms
## Psalm 91

The book of Psalms is found close to the middle of your Bible. It is a collection of the writings of several individuals stretching from the time of Moses to the Babylonian captivity. The Hebrew words for the book title means "the book of praises," while the Greek word that led to the English word means "songs." The book of Psalms has been divided into five books similar to the Pentateuch, the first five books of the Bible. The topics range from songs of praise and thanksgiving extolling God's character and power to prayers asking for God's forgiveness, deliverance, protection, and provision. The complete honesty of the authors continues to relate to mankind across the ages. They are used for drawing close to God in private devotions and in public worship services.

Read Psalm ninety-one in your Bible with your teacher and discuss its theme. Then reread the first two verses in the Kings James Version used for your Bible memory work. Discuss unfamiliar vocabulary, such as *refuge* and *fortress*, with the teacher. Begin learning the verses to recite on Friday.

### Discussion and Notebook Work

1. Use your Bible dictionary-concordance to record the definitions for *extol, refuge,* and *fortress.*

   ⋆ Read the related Scripture verses.
   ⋆ Use each one in a sentence to demonstrate your understanding.

2. Paraphrase Psalm 91:1–2 using the **paraphrase chart** and add each week's memory verses to it.

   (See the examples provided on the next page.)

| Verses | My Paraphrase |
|---|---|
| *Psalm 91:1* He who dwells in the shelter of the Most High will rest in the shadow of the Almighty.<br>*Psalm 91:2* | • He who belongs to God is sheltered from danger.<br>• |
| **Relate to My Life** | |
| *Psalm 91:1* God protects me from danger.<br>*Psalm 91:2* | |

3. List the seven kinds of psalms and give examples. If you need help, look at your Bible's introductory page for Psalms.

# The Book of Job
## Job 1, 2, 42

The book of Job is about a real man who suffered terribly. The book reveals the role of Satan as the source of Job's misery. It shows that God is sovereign (in control of everything), and willing and able to deliver His people when they cry out to Him. It records the conversations between Job and his friends trying to understand the reason why people—especially Godly people—suffer.

Read Job chapters one and two to identify the character of Job and the reason for his suffering.

### Discussion and Notebook Work

1. Use Webster's 1828 *Dictionary* to record the definition for *sovereign*.

2. Use a **T-chart** to record the internal and external character of Job as you read Job chapters one and two.

The Character of Job

| Internal | External |
|---|---|
| | |

3. Discuss how God's sovereignty is revealed in Job chapters one and two.

4. Participate in a **Readers Theatre activity** for Job chapters one, two, and forty-two.

**Wisdom Literature and Prophecy**

Wisdom comes from God.

# Ecclesiastes and the Song of Solomon
## Ecclesiastes 1, 3, 5

Wisdom comes from God.

The book of Ecclesiastes was written by King Solomon after reflecting upon his life. He began well by asking God to give him wisdom to rule the nation wisely, but at some point he went astray. Being a great and powerful king, he made many choices that led him into sin, pride, and self-indulgence. He experienced all that the world had to offer and found in the end that the most important thing in life was to, "Fear God and keep his commandments, for this is the whole duty of man." (Ecclesiastes 12:13b)

Every person has times when he is in a bad mood or happy mood or angry mood. You can often tell the mood of a person by his speech or behavior. Read Ecclesiastes 1:1–11 to find out how Solomon was feeling when he wrote the book of Ecclesiastes and discuss with your teacher the mood changes you see expressed in the verses.

In reading Ecclesiastes, you can learn common sense wisdom that pertains to living in this world and spiritual wisdom that leads to eternal life. Read Ecclesiastes 5:2–7 and discuss with your teacher what these verses mean and how the meaning affects your life.

The book of the Song of Solomon was also written by Solomon as a poetic conversation between himself and the young woman he loved. In the poem, Solomon is referred to as the bridegroom and the Shulamite woman as the bride. The story describes married love. There is another level of meaning for this text, however. Some scholars believe this book may serve the dual purpose of describing God's love for Israel and the Church. Read chapter three to identify the two levels of meaning.

### Discussion and Notebook Work
1. Use Webster's 1828 *Dictionary* and your Bible dictionary-concordance to complete a **word map** for *vow*.

2. Write a paragraph after reading Ecclesiastes 5:2–7 which explains how being careful with your speech can keep you from having trouble with people and with God. Give examples.

3. Read Ecclesiastes 3:1–8 and participate in a **Readers Theatre activity.**

# Proverbs
## Proverbs 1, 28

The book of Proverbs is the last of the books that is believed to have been written mostly by Solomon, but it also includes some proverbs written by others. According to Webster's 1828 *Dictionary*, a *proverb* is a wise saying "rich in practical truths and excellent rules for the conduct of all classes of men." In other words, the book of Proverbs is a collection of short moral truths with wisdom for every area of life. This is why it is included in the study of what we call *wisdom literature*.

The purpose of the book of Proverbs is found in verses two through six of the first chapter. To summarize from your Bible, the purpose is:

* To attain wisdom, discipline, and understanding
* To learn to do what is right, just, and fair
* To give prudence to the simple and knowledge and discretion to the young
* To add learning and guidance to the wise and discerning, who will listen
* To understand proverbs, parables, and the sayings and riddles of the wise

Verse seven of chapter one is a key to our understanding of the book, "The fear of the Lord is the beginning of knowledge, but fools despise wisdom and discipline." Webster's 1828 *Dictionary* provides several definitions for *wisdom*. The following are a couple of definitions that apply to our study of Proverbs:

* *wisdom*—the knowledge and fear of God
* *wisdom*—the right use or exercise of knowledge

A study of Proverbs goes hand in hand with the key principle taught in fourth grade, "How the Seed of Local Self-Government Is Planted." The Bible is the source of truth by which we live our lives. If we choose to obey God's rules, this is called Christian self-government. When these truths are lived out by self-governing individuals the *seed of local self-government is planted*. It is planted in the home, the church, the community, and the nation. When this happens, God will be honored in the public life by the laws the nation chooses and citizens will choose to obey those laws because of their own personal self-government under Christ.

Turn to Proverbs chapter twenty-eight and read the Scriptures to see examples of the righteous and the wicked contrasted.

God has given man the free will to choose to obey or not.

Local self-government

### Discussion and Notebook Work

1. Record the memory verses, Psalm 91:3–4, underneath Psalm 91:12 and file.

   "Surely he shall deliver thee from the snare of the fowler, and from the noisome pestilence. He shall cover thee with his feathers, and under his wings shalt thou trust: his truth shall be thy shield and buckler." (Psalm 91:3–4)

2. Practice the entire passage to recite later in the week.

3. Add the new memory verses to your **paraphrase chart.**

4. Use Webster's 1828 *Dictionary* to record the definitions for *prudence* and *discretion.*

5. Select verses in Proverbs chapter twenty-eight that are examples of the Principle, "How the Seed of Local Self-Government Is Planted." Record the verses.

6. Use a **T-chart** to compare and contrast the righteous and the wicked as you read Proverbs chapter twenty-eight.

## Instructions Concerning Self-Government
### Proverbs 10, 14, 16, 22, 26

> God has given man the free will to choose to obey or not.

Another word for self-government is *self-control.* Proverbs 25:28 in your NIV Adventure Bible says, "Like a city whose walls are broken down is a man who lacks self-control." The King James Version translates it this way, "He that hath no rule over his own spirit is like a city that is broken down, and without walls." This could be interpreted to mean that a person without self-control has no rules that he lives by to maintain a Godly standard of behavior. There are no guidelines by which he measures his conduct as to whether it is good or evil. Anything goes in his life. He is easily enticed to participate in foolish behavior by those without wisdom. The Word of God provides the walls of protection or fences one needs to stay on the road that leads to life rather than destruction.

Read the following Scriptures to glean wisdom in the behaviors that will bless or withhold blessing from your own life:

* Proverbs 10:2 (stealing)
* Proverbs 10:4–5 (laziness)
* Proverbs 14:23 (hard work)
* Proverbs 16:32 (controlling temper)
* Proverbs 22:24–25 (friends & associates)
* Proverbs 26:20 (gossip)

### Discussion and Notebook Work

1. Use your Bible dictionary-concordance to record the definition for *self-control*.
   * Read the related Scripture verses.
   * Write a sentence to demonstrate your understanding.
2. Complete a **paraphrase chart** by adding each of the proverbs from your reading.

| Verses | My Paraphrase |
|---|---|
| Relate to My Life | |

## Family Government
### Proverbs 3, 6, 13, 17, 23, 29

God has ordained families to be the structure through which His blessings flow in life. He has also provided instructions for the individuals within the family to maintain order and peace. The term *government* means control, restraint, and exercise of authority. To determine who is governing we sometimes ask the question, "Who or what is in control?" The government of the family under God flows from the father and mother to the children. Proverbs provides many words of wisdom about family life and what makes for happiness. Read the following Scriptures for the instructions that, if followed by all parties involved, make for a blessed and peaceful family life.

* Proverbs 3:11–12; 29:15,17 (discipline of son)
* Proverbs 6:20–22 (obeying the commands/teaching of parents)
* Proverbs 13:1 (a wise son)
* Proverbs 17:6 (pride in parents)
* Proverbs 23:22 (honor parents)

God has given man the free will to choose to obey or not.

### Discussion and Notebook Work

1. Use your Bible dictionary-concordance to record the definition for *ordain*. Write a sentence to demonstrate your understanding.
2. Reason from each proverb you read to write a sentence about how its message applies to your life.

# The Virtue of Honesty

God's Word is the standard by which we measure everything to determine whether it is truth. In John 14:6 Jesus said, "I am the way, the truth, and the life." Of the Holy Spirit, John 14:17 says that the Spirit of truth dwells in us. If we are to have fellowship with God, and represent Him to the world, we must be people who practice truth whether it is in word, deed, or business transactions. *Honesty* is a Christian virtue and is defined in Webster's 1828 *Dictionary* as "fairness, truth, upright conduct, and the practice of justice in moral transactions." Proverbs has much to say about honesty in different spheres of life. Read the following and receive instruction that will help you to walk according to the Spirit of truth.

- ★ Proverbs 11:1
- ★ Proverbs 17:23
- ★ Proverbs 20:14
- ★ Proverbs 21:6

### Discussion and Notebook Work

1. Record the definitions of unfamiliar vocabulary and use each word in a sentence.

2. Write the main point or idea for each proverb you read.

3. Use what you learned from your reading to write a paragraph telling about the importance of honesty.

# The Treatment of Enemies
## Isaiah 55; Proverbs 10, 16, 24, 25

God has given man the free will to choose to obey or not.

When Solomon asked God for wisdom and understanding in order to govern Israel with justice, he was asking for attributes of God's very own character. Isaiah 55:8–9 says, "'For my thoughts are not your thoughts, neither are your ways my ways,' declares the LORD. 'As the heavens are higher than the earth, so are my ways higher than your ways and my thoughts than your thoughts.'" Man's ways are often very different than God's ways. For example, God has called man to walk by faith in what God has said rather than what he sees. However, man walks in the natural by what he sees and understands.

Another example is that God's way of dealing with an enemy is the opposite of the way most people would handle conflict. In the New Testament, God instructs us to love our enemies. Remember, the Word tells us that God is love and that He loved us before we came to know and accept His love, while we were still His enemies.

Read the following proverbs to learn God's wisdom in responding to our enemies.

  ⋆ Proverbs 10:12          ⋆ Proverbs 24:17–18
  ⋆ Proverbs 16:7           ⋆ Proverbs 25:21–22

### Discussion and Notebook Work

1. Record the memory verses, Psalm 91:5–6, underneath Psalm 91:3–4 and file.

   "Thou shalt not be afraid for the terror by night; nor for the arrow that flieth by day; nor for the pestilence that walketh in darkness; nor for the destruction that wasteth at noonday." (Psalm 91:5–6)

2. Practice the entire passage to recite later in the week.

3. Add the new memory verses to the **paraphrase chart.**

4. Use your Bible dictionary-concordance to record the definition for *enemy*. Read the related Scripture verses.

5. Create and complete a page on the ways God tells us to deal with our enemies. (See the example given on the next page.)

| Proverbs | God's Way | Man's Way |
|---|---|---|
| Proverbs 10:12<br>Proverbs 16:7<br>Proverbs 24:17-18<br>Proverbs 25:21-22 | Love | Hateful |

6. Use the information from the chart to write a paragraph to relate how you would treat an enemy God's way.

# Wisdom Concerning Friends
## Proverbs 13, 17, 27

Unlike an enemy, it is easy to love a friend. According to Webster's 1828 *Dictionary*, a *friend* is "one who is attached to another by affection; one who entertains for another sentiments of esteem, respect and affection, which lead him to desire his company, and to seek to promote his happiness and prosperity; opposed to foe or enemy." It is important to choose friends wisely, since this person will likely be an influence upon you for good or for bad. You will also want to be able to trust this person with your innermost thoughts and feelings. Read the following verses about friends:

* Proverbs 13:20     * Proverbs 27:9
* Proverbs 17:9      * Proverbs 27:17
* Proverbs 17:17

### Discussion and Notebook Work

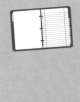

1. Use Webster's 1828 *Dictionary* and your Bible dictionary-concordance to record the definitions for *friend* and *friendship*. Read the related Scripture verses.

2. Use the definitions and verses on *friendship* to complete a **word map.**

3. Choose one verse that describes you as a friend and record why it applies to you.

# Bad Company
## Proverbs 1, 4, 9, 13, 22, 29

God has given man the free will to choose to obey or not.

The King James Bible advises in 1 Corinthians 15:33, "Do not be deceived: Bad company corrupts good morals." The same verse is translated this way in your Bible, "Do not be misled: 'Bad company corrupts good character.'" In the last lesson, you learned about what makes a good friend. In this lesson, the proverbs you read will give you instruction about the kinds of people you want to avoid when choosing your friends. Poor friends will influence you for evil and will cause hardship and difficulty for you. Think carefully as you read the following Scriptures. Ask yourself what you can do to avoid bad company.

* Proverbs 1:10–19 (thieves and murderers)
* Proverbs 4:14–15 (walking with the wicked)
* Proverbs 9:6 (the foolish)
* Proverbs 13:20 (the wise)
* Proverbs 22:24–25 (the angry)
* Proverbs 29:24 (the thief)

### Discussion and Notebook Work

1. Use your Bible dictionary-concordance to record the definitions for *entice* and *folly*.
   * Read the related Scripture verses.
   * Use *entice* and *folly* in sentences to demonstrate your understanding.
2. Choose a proverb from your reading and draw a picture that illustrates its meaning to you.
3. Write a paragraph summarizing what you can do to avoid bad company.

# The Mocker
## Proverbs 9, 13, 15, 21, 24

As you have seen, the book of Proverbs has great wisdom about the kind of company to keep. There is another type of person you will want to avoid choosing as a close friend—the mocker. The characteristics of a mocker, who may also be called a *scorner*, are described in the Webster's 1828 *Dictionary*. Turn to the definitions of *mocker* and *mockery* and read them before going on to read what Proverbs has to say about these people.

Read the following:

★ Proverbs 9:12
★ Proverbs 13:1, 13
★ Proverbs 15:12

★ Proverbs 21:11
★ Proverbs 24:9

### Discussion and Notebook Work

1. Complete a **vocabulary word analysis chart** for *mocker*.

2. Create and complete a page comparing the results of being a wise learner versus one who mocks wise teaching. (See the examples provided below.)

The Wise versus the Mocker

| Proverbs | Wise Learner | Mocker—Refusing to Learn |
|---|---|---|
| 9:12 | | |
| 13:1 A wise son heeds his father's instruction, but a mocker does not listen to rebuke. | Heeds instruction | Does not listen to advice |
| 13:13 | | |
| 15:12 | | |
| 21:11 | | |
| 24:9 | | |

3. Write a paragraph to summarize the blessings of being a wise learner.

# An Overview of Isaiah and His Messages
## Isaiah 6

An *overview* is a brief summary without a lot of detail. The lessons for this week will answer broad questions about the book of Isaiah (who, when, where, why, and what) as we study the prophecies of Scripture.

First of all, the book is written by the prophet Isaiah. A *prophet* according to Webster's 1828 *Dictionary* is a person "inspired or instructed by God to announce future events." In other words, a prophet delivers messages from God to people as he is directed by God. Prophets were not always received well by the people to whom God sent them. In fact, they were often rejected and persecuted, some suffering violent, unjust death because of the hardness of the peoples' hearts. It is traditionally believed that Isaiah met his death by being "sawn asunder." (Hebrews 11:37) It took a lot of courage to be a prophet in Old Testament times.

Isaiah was the son of Amoz. Isaiah's name means "Jehovah is salvation." Bible scholars differ on the exact dates of Isaiah's ministry, but most agree that he acted as a prophet to Israel for sixty years from around 740 B.C. to 680 B.C. His mission from God was to call Judah to repent of its sin and to return to God. This was during the time of the divided kingdom. You will remember that the Northern Kingdom was known as *Israel* and the Southern Kingdom was known as *Judah* (sometimes both kingdoms together are referred to simply as *Israel*). He warned the people of the coming judgment on their sins in the first section of the book, chapters 1–39. The second section comforts the suffering people and provides hope for them and descriptions of the coming Messiah.

Read about Isaiah's call to ministry in Isaiah 6:1–8.

### Discussion and Notebook Work

1. Record the memory verses, Psalm 91:7–8, underneath Psalm 91:5–6 and file.

   "A thousand shall fall at thy side, and ten thousand at thy right hand; but it shall not come nigh thee. Only with thine eyes shalt thou behold and see the reward of the wicked." (Psalm 91:7–8)

2. Practice the entire passage to recite later in the week.

3. Add the new memory verses to your **paraphrase chart.**

God's Principle of Individuality

God warns those He loves of judgment for sin.

4. Use your Bible dictionary-concordance to record the definition for *prophet*. Read the related Scripture verses.

5. Read the introductory page to survey the book of Isaiah in your Bible.

6. Begin a prophets **timeline** and continue throughout your study of the prophets.

7. Complete a **K-W-L chart** for Isaiah's commission using Isaiah 6:1–8.

# God's Patient Nature Revealed
## Isaiah 7, 9, 50, 53

You may remember that Israel began as a theocracy. Let's review: according to Webster's 1828 *Dictionary*, a *theocracy* means, "Government of a state by the immediate direction of God." Israel was governed by God speaking to the nation through His priests, prophets, and judges until the time Saul was appointed to be the first king. The form of government under a king is called a *monarchy*. A *monarchy*, according to Webster's 1828 *Dictionary* is, "A state or government in which the supreme power is lodged in the hands of a single person."

God disciplines those He loves.

At the time of Isaiah's ministry, Israel was a monarchy. Even though Israel had rejected God as their King, God did not forget His covenant with His chosen people, Israel. He expected the kings to rule according to His laws and to uphold the worship of the one and only true God. When they didn't obey and instead led the people into the worship of idols, God brought discipline through various means: one of them was Israel's invasion by foreign armies.

However, even when Israel rebelled, God still showed His love by sending prophets to the kings to call them back to Himself. Some believe that Isaiah was related to royalty or functioned as a scribe in the palace at Jerusalem. From Scripture, it is clear that Isaiah ministered as a prophet during the reigns of several kings.

You see, God had a plan to bring the Messiah through the people of Israel. Even though He allows judgment to come because of sin, He is still faithful to fulfill His promises; when we repent, God is merciful and lifts His just wrath from us. The Bible tells us that God disciplines those He loves (Revelation 3:19).

**Wisdom Literature and Prophecy**

God revealed His plan for the redemption of mankind through the prophecies of Isaiah. Read Isaiah 9:6–7. This is a description of the eternal King (who is Jesus) and the government of His eternal kingdom.

Read Isaiah 53, which describes the suffering, death, and burial of the future Messiah and King—Jesus.

### Discussion and Notebook Work

1. Identify the names of King Jesus listed in Isaiah 9:6 and write a sentence for each name telling how Jesus' character is revealed in that name.

2. Note the Old Testament prophecies about Jesus in Isaiah and trace their fulfillment in the New Testament:

   - Read the Scriptures below.
   - Summarize the prophecy.
   - Create and complete a page for your work similar to the one below (see the example provided).

| Prophecy in Isaiah | Fulfillment in New Testament |
|---|---|
| Isaiah 7:14<br>*A virgin will give birth to a son named Immanuel.* | Luke 1:26–27, 30–31<br>*Mary gave birth to Jesus.* |
| Isaiah 9:1–2 | Matthew 4:13–16 |
| Isaiah 50:6 | Matthew 26:67 |
| Isaiah 53:3 | John 1:11<br>Luke 23:18 |
| Isaiah 53:5 | Romans 5:6, 8 |
| Isaiah 53:9 | Matthew 27:57–60 |
| Isaiah 53:12 | Mark 15:27–28 |

**Wisdom Literature and Prophecy**

# Choices Have Consequences
## Isaiah 3

The word *consequence* means the result or effect that is produced from an action or actions. In other words, our choices result in many of the events in our lives whether they are good or bad.

Read Isaiah chapter three to learn the consequences that came to Jerusalem and Judah because of their sin.

### Discussion and Notebook Work

1. Use your Bible dictionary-concordance to read the definition for *judgment*. Read the related Scriptures.

2. Complete a **concept/definition map** for *judgment*.

3. Look back over what you read to identify the things that God said caused the fall of Jerusalem and Judah and record your findings.

4. Relate a good or bad consequence to a choice you made in your life and record.

# Choose God Rather than Idols
## Isaiah 44

Isaiah is given a message to speak to Israel (referring to both the Northern and Southern Kingdoms) from God about their idolatry. It is written in the first person as God speaks directly to the people. God mocks them for thinking the very idols they make with their own hands can do anything for them.

Read Isaiah 44:6–22. Look for the types of idols the people were making and worshipping.

### Discussion and Notebook Work

1. Use your Bible dictionary-concordance to record the definition for *idol*. Read the related Scripture verses.

2. Complete a **K-W-L chart** on idol worship using Isaiah chapter forty-four.

3. Write a paragraph summarizing what you learned about idol worship. (Hint: Is there anything in your life that you value more than God?)

# An Overview of Jeremiah and His Messages
## Jeremiah 1

The ministry of the prophet Jeremiah to Israel came after Isaiah's. Most scholars agree that Jeremiah's ministry was from about 626 B.C. to 586 B.C. and was mainly to Judah and its capital city, Jerusalem (the Southern Kingdom). However, Jeremiah often refers to Israel (the Southern and Northern Kingdoms combined).

The first chapter of Jeremiah tells about his individuality and unique call to ministry. God called Jeremiah to be a prophet to Judah to plead with the people to repent of their sins and turn back to God to avoid judgment.

Jeremiah's message did not make him a popular person. In fact, most of the people, the kings of Judah, and even his friends and family rejected him and

God disciplines those He loves.

his messages from God. Besides being poor, he was imprisoned, thrown in a well, and taken by force to Egypt. In today's world, he would not be considered a successful person. We may think that success is a good job, lots of money and nice things, lots of friends, and good looks. In God's eyes, you are successful when you are obedient to Him. Read Jeremiah 1:1–8 to understand Jeremiah's call to be a prophet. When did God know Jeremiah and set him apart to be a prophet?

### Discussion and Notebook Work

1. Record the memory verses, Psalm 91:9–10, underneath Psalm 91:7–8 and file.

   "Because thou hast made the LORD, which is my refuge, even the most High, thy habitation; there shall no evil befall thee, neither shall any plague come nigh thy dwelling." (Psalm 91:9–10)

2. Practice the entire passage to recite later in the week.

3. Add the new memory verses to the **paraphrase chart.**

4. Read the introductory pages to the book of Jeremiah.

5. After reading Jeremiah 1:1–8, create a page similar to the one below and complete your answers to the following questions using the Scripture verses:

### The Call of Jeremiah and Other Prophets

| Questions | Jeremiah | Moses | Ezekiel |
|-----------|----------|-------|---------|
| What did God appoint the prophet to do? | Jeremiah 1:5 | Exodus 3:10 | Ezekiel 2:3–4 |
| What did the prophet think about this request? | Jeremiah 1:6 | Exodus 4:10 | Ezekiel 3:14–15 |
| What did God speak to the prophet? | Jeremiah 1:7–8 | Exodus 12:11–12 | Ezekiel 3:17, 22 |

6. Write a paragraph relating ways you can serve God today.

7. Add Jeremiah to your prophets **timeline.**

# Jeremiah's Relationship with God
## Jeremiah 12, 18, 20

God hates sin and must judge it.

The New Testament is a record of the new covenant we have with God through Jesus Christ. Because He died for our sins, we can go directly to God in prayer and have a relationship with Him. Yet we see many people who had an intimate relationship with God under the old covenant practices.

Through the record of Jeremiah's books (Jeremiah and Lamentations) we learn that he was not afraid to tell God how he was really feeling about things. Whether he was distressed and fearful or angry about the injustices he saw, he talked to God about it. Through prayer, Jeremiah learned about God and His ways.

Read the following passages to learn how Jeremiah was feeling at the time: Jeremiah 12:1–2, 18:18–20, and 20:7–10.

Later, God answered Jeremiah. God will answer you as well if you go to Him in prayer with all of your concerns. Jeremiah 29:11–14a is a favorite passage for many people. "'For I know the plans I have for you,' declares the LORD, 'plans to prosper you and not to harm you, plans to give you hope and a future. Then you will call upon me and come and pray to me, and I will listen to you. You will seek me and find me when you seek me with all your heart. I will be found by you,' declares the LORD.'" In the New Testament, Luke 11:9 says, "Ask and it will be given to you; seek and you will find; knock and the door will be opened to you." Learning to hear from God is a process that takes practice and being willing to be quiet to listen. Just like your friends, God wants to have a part in the conversation too.

### Discussion and Notebook Work

1. Use Webster's 1828 *Dictionary* to record the definition for *success*.

2. Read the related Scriptures to determine the rules of success according to God and record what you learn.

   ★ Joshua 1:7–9                    ★ Philippians 1:20–21
   ★ Matthew 6:32–34              ★ Philippians 3:13–14
   ★ Galatians 6:9

3. Create and complete a page to summarize Jeremiah's complaints and God's responses similar to the one below.

| Jeremiah's Complaints | God's Responses |
|---|---|
| Jeremiah 12:1–2 | |
| Jeremiah 18:18–20 | |
| Jeremiah 20:7–10 | |

4. Write a paragraph in the form of a prayer telling God how you feel about a situation in your life.

5. File the song "What a Friend We Have in Jesus" in your notebook and sing it as your teacher leads you.

# God's Opinion of False Religion
## Jeremiah 7

God judges sin.

Are you beginning to understand how much God desires to have a relationship with His people? He doesn't want an empty external show with no real heart commitment to Him. The people of Jeremiah's day went to the temple to worship the Lord because they felt like they had to, but their hearts were far from Him. You could call them *hypocrites*. The Webster's 1828 *Dictionary* defines *hypocrite* as, "One who feigns to be what he is not; one who has the form of godliness without the power, or who assumes an appearance of piety and virtue, when he is destitute of true religion."

100                    **Wisdom Literature and Prophecy**

Jeremiah knew that God was going to allow the Temple to be destroyed one day because of the people's sin. Last unit we learned that God lives in His people now, not in a beautiful building like the Temple. Every Christian is the temple of the Holy Spirit.

Read Jeremiah 7:1–11 to discover what the people of Israel were doing that God said would bring judgment.

## Discussion and Notebook Work

1. Use your Bible dictionary-concordance to record the definition for *hypocrite*. Read the related Scripture verses.

2. After reading Jeremiah 7:1–11, use a **T-chart** to identify the righteous actions God says He will honor and record them.

| Actions God Will Judge | Actions God Will Honor |
|---|---|
| Trusting deceptive words (v. 4) | *Trust in God* |
| Treating others unjustly (v. 5) | *Justice* |
| Oppressing the alien (foreigner), the fatherless, and the widow (v. 6) | |
| Shedding of blood (v. 6) | |
| Stealing, murder, adultery, perjury, and worshipping false gods (v. 9) | |
| Standing before God and choosing to continue to sin (v. 10) | |

3. Read Jeremiah 7:19 and write a paragraph answering the question, "Who gets hurt when we turn away from God?"

# Prophecy of the Coming Messiah
## Jeremiah 23, 31, 33

From studying Isaiah and Jeremiah, you have seen that prophets don't just talk about future things. They talk to the people about how they are supposed to live and worship. Prophets call people to obey God and to treat each other with justice and righteousness. Remember the first and second commandments are to love God with all your heart, soul, and mind, and to love your neighbor as yourself (Matthew 22:36–39).

Like Isaiah, Jeremiah also prophesied about the coming Messiah. Christians know that the prophecies of a coming Messiah were fulfilled in the life, death, and resurrection of Jesus Christ.

### Discussion and Notebook Work

1. Use your Bible dictionary-concordance to record the definition for *Messiah*. Read the related Scripture verse.

2. Read Jeremiah 23:5–6 to identify and record the names that refer to the Messiah.

3. Complete a **concept/definition map** for *Messiah*.

4. Read Jeremiah 31:31–34, summarize and describe God's relationship with His people under the new covenant or *New Testament*. Record your thoughts.

5. Read Jeremiah 33:4–16, summarize and record what God promised to Judah and Israel.

**Wisdom Literature and Prophecy**

# An Overview of Ezekiel and His Messages
## Ezekiel 1–2, 33; 2 Kings 24

From studying Jeremiah, you may remember that Jeremiah 1:5 says, "Before I formed you in the womb I knew you, before you were born I set you apart; I appointed you as a prophet to the nations." Psalm 139 also speaks of God creating each of us in our mother's womb and our days being written in His book before we were ever born. This tells us how involved He really is in our lives and our purpose. God providentially places His servants and prepares them for their calling.

God's hand can also be seen in the life of the prophet Ezekiel, the son of Buzi, a Zadokite priest. Being born into a priestly family meant he would be trained as a priest as well. However, he was taken captive as a young man in 597 B.C. from Judah and sent to Babylon. Ezekiel received his call to be a prophet to the exiled Jews in Babylon. God allowed him to live through this tragedy so that he could be God's mouthpiece to explain the judgment and to bring His peace, courage, and hope to Israel. Ezekiel's name means "God strengthens." As you study the book of Ezekiel, you will come to understand that God indeed strengthened him.

By reading Ezekiel 1:1–3, we can guess when Ezekiel prophesied. We read that he received his call in the thirtieth year, which was also the fifth year of the exile of Judah's King Jehoiachin. This may mean that Ezekiel was thirty years old, the age when Old Testaments priests began ministry. The time frame of the exile means his ministry as a prophet began around 593 B.C. and continued until about 571 B.C. by most accounts.

Read Ezekiel 1:1–3 to understand the setting of the book. Locate Babylon on your Bible map. Read 2 Kings 24:14–17 for an account of the taking away of the people of Jerusalem to Babylon.

### Discussion and Notebook Work

1. Record the memory verses, Psalm 91:11–12, underneath Psalm 91:9–10 and file.
   "For he shall give his angels charge over thee, to keep thee in all thy ways. They shall bear thee up in their hands, lest thou dash thy foot against a stone." (Psalm 91:11–12)

2. Practice the entire passage to recite later in the week.

God hates sin and must judge it.

3. Add the new memory verses to the **paraphrase chart.**

4. Read Ezekiel chapter two.

   ★ Locate three adjectives that describe the people of the nation to whom God is sending Ezekiel.
   ★ Use your Webster's 1828 *Dictionary* to record the definitions for the adjectives.
   ★ Write a sentence with each adjective to demonstrate your understanding.
   ★ Record the three things in nature God that likens the people to.
   ★ What did the vision of the scroll represent to Ezekiel in verses nine and ten?

5. Use your Bible dictionary-concordance to define *lament, mourning,* and *woe.*

   ★ Read the related Scriptures.
   ★ Write a sentence using each word to demonstrate your understanding.
   ★ What do you think these words have to do with Ezekiel's message to the people?

6. Add Ezekiel to the prophets **timeline.**

# Called to Be a Watchman
## Ezekiel 3, 33

God clarified Ezekiel's call in Ezekiel 3:16–21. God called him a *watchman.* Cities in Bible times were surrounded by high, thick walls to protect the city from enemies. Men took turns standing on the walls to watch both day and night for enemy armies and to sound an alarm if they saw any coming. Watchmen are also seen in Scripture doing a policeman's job patrolling to preserve the peace and order of the city. In the last unit you studied Nehemiah and learned about how some of the people worked to rebuild the city walls of Jerusalem while others watched for the enemy.

Read Ezekiel 3:16–21 to discover the duties of God's spiritual watchman and the seriousness of that responsibility. Isn't this a part of what Christian's are supposed to do? If you love your neighbor as yourself, you would want to warn him of any danger.

### Discussion and Notebook Work

1. Use your Webster's 1828 *Dictionary* to record the definition for *watchman*.

2. Use your thesaurus to find several other words that are synonyms for *watchman* and use each one in a sentence.

3. After reading Ezekiel 3:16–21, record the three *W's* that describe the duties of a watchman.

4. Describe the seriousness of the responsibilities of a watchman.

5. Read Ezekiel 33:1–9 to learn more about the watchman's job and answer these questions.

   a. How does the watchman of the land warn the people that the sword of the enemy is coming?

   b. What responsibility do the people of the land have when the watchman sounds the alarm?

# The Uniqueness of Ezekiel's Ministry
## Ezekiel 12

So many times people are unhappy with whom God made them to be. Especially in today's culture, there is a lot of pressure to think, look, act, and dress just like everybody else. Some will even turn away from God if other people think that being a Christian isn't cool. Second Corinthians 10:12 warns believers that it is not wise to compare ourselves with others.

Remember, God's Principle of Individuality teaches us that each person is created in the image of God and given unique internal and external identity that is of special value to God. We see the individuality of Ezekiel in the way he brought God's messages to the people. Because God knew Ezekiel's talents and personality (just like He knows us), He communicated with Ezekiel in a special way that he would understand. The way God told Ezekiel to deliver each message was based on who Ezekiel was and the people the message was intended for.

Ezekiel delivered some of his messages to the people living in Babylon by symbolic actions. Today, we call this *pantomime*. God told Ezekiel exactly what to do to communicate to the exiled people in Babylon the fall and exile of

God hates sin and must judge it.

those Jews still living in Jerusalem. This is described in Ezekiel 12:1–16. Read this portion of Scripture and imagine how the people must have responded as Ezekiel was acting out God's message to the people.

### Discussion and Notebook Work

1. Use Webster's 1828 *Dictionary* to record the definition for *pantomime*.

2. Participate in a **Readers Theatre activity** using Ezekiel 12:1–16 by reading and performing for your classmates using your best oral reading skills.

3. Illustrate the exile as described in Ezekiel chapter twelve.

# Prophecy of the Restoration of the Nation
## Ezekiel 37

God sends
prophets to
warn people
of sin because
of His great
love.

Ezekiel was faithful to deliver God's Word to His exiled people in Babylon about the destruction of Jerusalem because of the sins of the people. He also brought the word that judgment would come on the foreign nations for their own sins. Even though God allowed heathen (sinful) nations to defeat Israel and carry them into slavery, God also promised to judge their own evil ways. The conclusion of Ezekiel's ministry brought hope to the Israelites that they would be restored to God.

Read Ezekiel 37:15–28 to discover Ezekiel's message of hope, his symbolic act, and the future of the nation.

### Discussion and Notebook Work

1. Use your Bible dictionary-concordance to record the definitions for *symbol* and *restore*. Read the related Scripture verses.

2. Complete a **vocabulary word analysis chart** for *restore*.

3. Summarize in a paragraph the meaning of Ezekiel's symbolic act and the future of the nation.

4. Reason with your teacher about the following:

   a. What does it mean to be "in unity"?

   b. Why was it important that unity be restored to the nation?

5. Summarize the message in Ezekiel 37:1–15 about the valley of dry bones.

# An Overview of the Minor Prophets, Hosea and Micah, and Their Messages
## Hosea 1, 11; 1 Kings 12

We now turn our study of prophecy to the writings of the minor prophets. The word *minor* does not mean that these prophets are less important than the others: it just means that their books are not as long as the books of the major prophets. However, the messages of the minor prophets are just as important and powerful.

The first of the minor prophets we will study is Hosea, whose name means "salvation." In Hosea 1:1, we learn when Hosea ministered based on the reigns of the kings of Judah and Israel. Read this verse to see if you are familiar with any of the kings during the time that Hosea prophesied. God gave Hosea a message for the Northern Kingdom (or Israel). Scholars tell us that his ministry lasted from around 750 B.C. to 520 B.C., when a series of very wicked kings ruled Israel.

Because the kingdom of Israel had been divided, the kings of Israel (the Northern Kingdom) did not want their people going back to Jerusalem in the Southern Kingdom to worship. So Jeroboam, the first king of Israel, told the people to worship two golden calves, saying that they were the ones who had brought Israel out of Egypt. This story is found in 1 Kings 12:26–29. Most of the kings after that followed in the worship of these false gods. The introducing of idol worship broke covenant with God and brought further sin and further judgment.

The book of Hosea is unusual in that it starts out by likening the unfaithfulness of Israel to God to the unfaithfulness of Hosea's own wife to him. The message of the book is that God's love is patient and even though He must discipline sin, His desire is to restore the relationship with His people. Read Hosea chapter eleven.

> God disciplines those He loves.

### Discussion and Notebook Work

1. Record the memory verses, Psalm 91:13–14, underneath Psalm 91:11–12 and file.

    "Thou shalt tread upon the lion and adder: the young lion and the dragon shalt thou trample under feet. Because he hath set his love upon me, therefore

will I deliver him: I will set him on high, because he hath known my name."
(Psalm 91:13–14)

2. Practice the entire passage to recite later in the week.

3. Add the new memory verse to the **paraphrase chart.**

4. Record and answer the reason questions from the reading of Hosea chapter eleven.

   a. What are some specific ways God says He blessed Israel?
   b. What was revealed about God's character?

5. Read Hosea 4:1–3 and reason what would be the most important right things for you to do as a Christian.

6. Add Hosea to the prophets **timeline.**

# The Hope of Restoration
## Hosea 13–14

God hates sin and must judge it.

You have seen in our studies this year that God is merciful. When His people sin, judgment comes; but with repentance, God forgives and restores the people to Himself. We see this same message in Hosea. Read Hosea chapter fourteen to understand that God continues to love His people even when His people are unfaithful.

Perhaps the sins of Israel appear far from your own life. But let's think a minute about their sin: they turned to other nations for help and to their idols instead of God. They did these things because they did not want to obey God. They wanted to do things their own way. Have you ever hardened your heart against God when you did not want to obey His Word?

### Discussion and Notebook Work

1. God uses similes to describe how He will heal the waywardness of Israel. Identify the similes in Hosea 14:5–8 to discover the way God promises to restore the people of Israel. Create a page similar to the following example to record your findings.

# Repentance Brings Blessings

| Scripture Verses from Hosea 14:5–8 | God's Promise of Restoration |
|---|---|
| v. 5 *"I will be like the dew to Israel; He will blossom like a lily. Like a cedar of Lebanon he will send down his roots;"* | • *Blossom like a lily*<br>•<br>• |
| v. 6 | |
| v. 7 | |
| v. 8 | |

2. Write and record a couple of similes of your own or search Hosea chapter thirteen for other similes.

3. Use Webster's 1828 *Dictionary* to record the definitions for *return*. (Focus on the second and sixth definitions.)

4. Write a paragraph telling about when you returned from your waywardness and the resulting blessings that followed.

# The Ministry and Message of Micah
## Micah 1–3

God raised up Micah as a prophet to Judah and Israel around the same time as Isaiah. Scholars don't agree on the exact dates of his ministry, but it appears his ministry was from around 740 B.C. to 690 B.C. Micah 1:1 identifies his hometown as Moresheth, a town in Judah near Jerusalem. One of his messages found in Micah chapter two shows a familiar pattern pointing out the sin, telling of the judgment, and then promising future deliverance.

God disciplines us for sin because He loves us.

In the second chapter of Micah, the message Micah delivered is given as if God is speaking (first person) directly to Judah. The first few verses talk about a man plotting evil. One is reminded that God knows our thoughts and that nothing is hidden from Him. Matthew 15:19–20 says, "For out of the heart come evil thoughts, murder, adultery, sexual immorality, theft, false testimony, slander. These are what make a man 'unclean.'" Read Micah 2:1–3 to see what the evil man was plotting and to learn what God will do to those who plan evil.

Also, at this time the prophets (as well as the rulers and leaders) were doing whatever was right in their own eyes. Read Micah chapter three to see what God says to these people.

### Discussion and Notebook Work

1. Use your Bible dictionary-concordance to define *iniquity, defraud, plot, rebuke,* and *bribe.*

   ★ Read the related Scripture verses.

   ★ Write sentences using each word to demonstrate your understanding.

2. Participate in a **Readers Theatre activity** by reading aloud Micah chapter two and performing for your classmates using your best oral reading skills.

3. Record the things that God called evil in Micah 2:1–3.

4. After reading Micah chapter three, create a page to record God's rebuke of the leaders and prophets (see the example provided).

### Leaders and Prophets Rebuked in Micah Three

| Injustices of Leaders and Prophets | God's Rebuke |
| --- | --- |
| 3:1–2 *The leaders hate good and love evil.* | 3:4 *God will not answer them and will hide His face from them.* |
| 3:5 | 3:6–7 |
| 3:9–11 | 3:12 |

5. Using the information you learned from this lesson, relate how you would conduct yourself as a leader.

6. Add Micah to the prophets **timeline.**

**Wisdom Literature and Prophecy**

# The Righteous Judge Presents His Case for Judgment
## Micah 5–6

God hates sin and must judge it.

It is amazing to think that the God of all creation speaks to mankind and that He reasons and pleads with us to turn from our wicked ways. He so loves us and wants us to love Him in return. It reminds me of the love of a parent for a child. The parent wants to bless his child in every way possible, enjoys being with the child, and never wants any harm to come to the child. Yet, when the child disobeys, especially repeatedly, the parent must discipline for the child's own good. If you can understand it, our heavenly Father loves us even more than our earthly fathers. Both make judgments that bring pain into our lives with the hope that correction will show us that we need to change our behavior.

In Micah chapter six, we find our heavenly Father acting as Judge and presenting His case against Judah by reminding them of things He has done for them. Micah 6:8 tells clearly what God expects of man. Then God proceeds to let the people know they are about to get a whipping. He makes it clear what they have done wrong so they know that God's punishment is just. Then He tells them what the punishment will be. Read this chapter and then complete the notebook work.

### Discussion and Notebook Work

1. Use your Bible dictionary-concordance to define *righteous* and *redeemed*.
   * Read the related Scripture verses.
   * Write sentences using the words you defined to demonstrate your understanding.

2. List some sins that brought discipline to God's children.

3. Write a paragraph relating Micah 6:8 to your own life.

4. Micah 6:14–15 has statements that seem to be contradictory. Create a page like the following example to record your explanation.

## Israel's Punishment, Micah 6:14–15

| Contradictory Statements | Explanation |
| --- | --- |
| v. 14<br>• *You will eat but not be satisfied; your stomach will still be empty.*<br>• *You will store up but save nothing, because what you save I will give to the sword.*<br>v. 15<br>• *You will plant but not harvest.*<br>• *You will press olives but not use the oil on yourselves.*<br>• *You will crush grapes but not drink the wine.* | • *You'll eat but never be full.*<br><br>•<br><br><br>•<br><br>•<br><br><br>• |

5. Read Micah 5:1–5 and look for clues that describe the future ruler of Judah/Israel. List the clues you find, and tell whom the clues are about and how you know who it is.

# An Overview of the Minor Prophets, Habakkuk and Zephaniah, and Their Messages
## Habakkuk 1; Zephaniah 12, 18, 20

**God judges sin.**

We have no information about Habakkuk except that the book of Habakkuk was probably written around 612 B.C. This would have made his ministry to Judah around the same time as Jeremiah's ministry. It's interesting to see that the two prophets both had questions for God. They weren't afraid to ask Him about why the wicked prosper, and why cruel, idolatrous nations were allowed to destroy more righteous nations, and other difficult questions like that.

God always answers us when we take our concerns to Him, but not always in the way we want or expect. In this case, God tells Habakkuk that He is raising up the Babylonians to bring judgment on Judah. Habakkuk chapter one contains of this discussion between Habakkuk and God; read it and note the figurative language the writer uses.

### Discussion and Notebook Work

1. Record the memory verses, Psalm 91:15–16, underneath Psalm 91:13–14 and file.

   "He shall call upon me, and I will answer him: I will be with him in trouble; I will deliver him, and honour him. With long life will I satisfy him, and shew him my salvation." (Psalm 91:15–16)

2. Practice the entire passage to recite later in the week.

3. Continue to add the new memory verses to the **paraphrase chart.**

4. Use Webster's 1828 *Dictionary* and your Bible dictionary-concordance to define *injustice* and *strife*. Read the related Scripture verses.

5. From the reading of Habakkuk chapter one:

   ★ Identify and record the adjectives and phrases that describe the Babylonians.

   ★ Use Webster's 1828 *Dictionary* and Bible dictionary-concordance to define these adjectives.

6. Reason and record why God chose Babylon to bring judgment on Judah.

7. Record the word picture Habakkuk uses in his second complaint about the nation God had chosen to bring judgment (Habakkuk 1:14–17).

*Enrichment activity*—Identify the main complaints of Jeremiah and Habakkuk from the Scriptures (Jeremiah 12:1–2, 18:18–20, 20:7–10; Habakkuk 1:2–4, 12–17). Record and answer the reason questions.

a. How are these complaints alike?

b. What is the basic theme of their complaints?

## God Answers Habakkuk Again
### Habakkuk 2–3

Y ou will find God's answer to Habakkuk's second question in chapter two. The chapter begins with Habakkuk stating, "I will stand at my watch and station myself on the ramparts; I will look to see what he will say to me, and what answer I am to give to this complaint." This implies that

God's answer did not come right away. We often think God does not answer us when we pray, but the real truth is that we don't wait and listen long enough to hear what He wants to say to us. Also, our ears are not in tune enough to recognize it when God is speaking to us. Habakkuk was willing to watch—to position himself to look—for the answer that was coming and to prepare his answer. Remember the discussion of the watchman a few lessons back? This is what the watchman does: he gets the mind of the Lord to report to the people by persistently seeking God until he hears from Him.

Read Habakkuk chapter two and answer the questions in your notebook.

### Discussion and Notebook Work

1. Use Webster's 1828 *Dictionary* and your Bible dictionary-concordance to define *hear* and *faith*. Read the related Scriptures verses.

2. Copy and answer the reason questions.

   a. Why did God want His answer recorded?
   b. What does God reveal about the timing of what He is about to say?
   c. Who is God speaking about in Habakkuk 2:7–8?
   d. How does God feel about the nation He is discussing?

3. God pronounced five woes upon the nation that He allowed to judge Israel in Habakkuk chapter two. Create a page similar to the one below to record the woes and judgment.

**God hates sin and must judge it.**

#### The Five Woes to Israel's Oppressor

| The Injustices—Habakkuk Two | Paraphrase God's Judgment |
|---|---|
| 2:6 *Extortion* | 2:7 *You will become a victim.* |
| 2:9 | 2:10 |
| 2:12 *Violence and crime* | 2:13 |
| 2:15 | 2:16 *Shame and disgrace will be yours.* |
| 2:19 *Idolatry* | 2:19 |

4. Record and answer the reason questions from Habakkuk chapter three:

   a. What word describes "the times" in verse 17?
   b. Identify the names of God in the chapter.
   c. Habakkuk says God makes his feet like the feet of a deer and enables him to go on the heights. What does this mean?
   d. How was Habakkuk's prayer to be communicated?

5. Add Habakkuk to the prophets **timeline.**

# God Must Judge Sin
## Zephaniah 1

God warns of sin because He loves us.

The prophet you will learn about today is named *Zephaniah,* meaning "God hides." Read Zephaniah 1:1 to learn about his heritage. This verse also reveals that he ministered to Judah during the reign of Josiah around 640 B.C. We can't be sure why his parents named him something that means "God hides," but we do know that God made Zephaniah a prophet and gave him this word to speak. The Bible tells us in Amos 3:7 that, "Surely the Sovereign LORD does nothing without revealing his plan to his servants the prophets." God reveals his truth to His prophets when He wants to for His purposes. The word given to Zephaniah was about future events, some of which were close at hand and others were far off. In fact, some of the things revealed to Zephaniah have not occurred yet. However, the prophecies in the Bible have all come to pass in the appropriate time ordained by God. We can absolutely trust this.

Zephaniah's heritage seems to indicate that his great, great grandfather was King Hezekiah, who was a good king in Judah. However, Hezekiah's son Manasseh was wicked, as was Amon after him. Then came King Josiah who repented and led God's people back to Him. God withheld judgment from Israel because of Josiah's repentance. Josiah made Godly decrees like removing idols from the land, commanding the reading of God's Word, and reinstituting the worship of God. The prophets of the day—Jeremiah, Zephaniah, and others—were perhaps influential in bringing about these reforms.

According to Zephaniah, many people in Israel obeyed the religious decrees externally but without any real change of heart towards God. Zephaniah was an instrument of God to deliver the message that judgment was coming. Read Zephaniah chapter one and complete the assigned notebook work.

### Discussion and Notebook Work

1. Use Webster's 1828 *Dictionary* to record the definitions for *reform* as a noun and as a verb.

2. From the reading of Zephaniah chapter one:

**Wisdom Literature and Prophecy**     115

* Identify and record Judah and Jerusalem's sins that God was going to judge.
* Discuss and compare the sins of Judah and Jerusalem to the sins of our nation today.

3. Add Zephaniah to the prophets **timeline.**

# The God of Justice and Grace
## Zephaniah 3

God hates sin.

From studying the prophecies of Scripture, you should have learned that God is consistent. This means that He is faithful. He does not lie. If He says He will do something, He does it. Looking back on history, we know that He did judge Judah, as He said He would. Yet He showed them grace by later returning His people to the land He had promised them after they were scattered into foreign lands by the invading armies.

We see God's judgment and grace described in Zephaniah chapter three. The chapter begins by telling Jerusalem's sins that God was going to judge. This is contrasted starting in verse 9 with God's grace to the people. *Grace* means favor or good treatment you do not deserve. This is one of the things God did for us when He sent Jesus to die for our sins.

There were four kinds of leaders in Jerusalem God identified here who deserved the coming punishment for their sins. They were officials, rulers, prophets, and priests. Not everyone who is in authority is a righteous person: nevertheless, according to Romans chapter thirteen, authorities are established by God and we are to obey them unless they tell us to disobey God. God will bring judgment on those authorities who are wicked.

When God's people go through severe trials, those trials purify them and bring them closer to God. We see that in this chapter as God describes the character of those He'll bring back to the city.

Read Zephaniah chapter three and complete the chart below showing what God will remove from the people of Jerusalem and what He will restore to them.

### Discussion and Notebook Work

1. Use your Bible dictionary-concordance to record the definition for *grace*. Read the related Scriptures.

2. From the reading of Zephaniah chapter three, create and complete a page identifying the things God will remove from the people and the things He will restore to the people of Jerusalem.

#### The Future of Jerusalem

| Removed from Jerusalem | Restored to Jerusalem |
|---|---|
|  |  |

3. Have you ever seen some difficult thing you have gone through actually turn out for your good? Maybe your character was refined by the experience. Think of an example you can share and write a paragraph about it.

# The Physical Geography of the Holy Land

The land God gave to the people of Israel is called by different names. In the Old Testament, God first told Abraham to leave his home to go to a land that God was going to show him, the land was called *Canaan*. It's also referred to as the *land of promise* in Hebrews 11:9 and other places in the Bible, so you may see some maps labeled the Promise Land. Other places in Scripture call this land *Palestina* (Exodus 15:14 and Isaiah 14:29, 31). It is often called *Palestine* today. The borders of the Holy Land have varied over the course of history.

Review *The Noah Plan®* Map Standard for physical maps before you begin the physical map of the Holy Land.

## Discussion and Notebook Work

1. Review the memory verses, Psalm 91:1–16, for final recitation later in the week and file.

2. Complete the map of the sites below according to *The Noah Plan* Map Standard.

   ★ Seas
      ★ Mediterranean Sea
      ★ Dead Sea (Salt Sea)
      ★ Sea of Galilee (*Chinnerath* in Old Testament)
   ★ Rivers
      ★ Jordan River
      ★ Jabbok River
      ★ Kishon River
      ★ Yarmuk River
   ★ Mountains
      ★ Mount Hermon
      ★ Mount Tabor
      ★ Mount Gerizim
      ★ Mount of Olives
      ★ Mount Carmel

# New Testament History

# The Early Church
## Acts 1

This unit we will study New Testament history. Refer to your overview to learn the topics you will be studying. Take a moment to locate the book of Acts in your Bible. The book of Acts, written by Luke, the physician and apostle, tells how the New Testament church began. The book is a record of the events that happened after the crucifixion and resurrection of Jesus through to the imprisonment of Paul in Rome, from about 30 A.D. to 60 A.D.

Read Acts 1:2 in your Bible: it refers to the day Jesus was taken up to heaven. You may have learned sometime that this event is called the *Ascension*. In verse three, Luke says that Jesus was seen by His disciples for forty days before the Ascension, proving to them again and again that He was alive. Jesus instructed them during this time not to leave Jerusalem until they were baptized with the Holy Spirit. He told His disciples that they would receive power to be His witnesses after they received the Holy Spirit. He said they would tell about Him in Jerusalem, Judea, Samaria, and all over the earth. This was like saying, "You will tell the Good News to your neighborhood, to people in your city, to those different from you in the next state, and even other countries where the people speak a different language and have different customs you couldn't begin to know." The disciples needed the power of the Holy Spirit to accomplish this enormous task!

Read Acts 1:12–26 to discover what important matter of business needed to be taken care of after the Ascension of Jesus. The casting of lots is a practice referred to in determining the mind of the Lord, but it is never done again in the Bible after the Holy Spirit came on the disciples. See *lot* in your Webster's 1828 *Dictionary* for further information. Also ask your teacher to explain the use of lots by the priests in the Old Testament.

In Acts 1:14 in your Bible, it says that they "all joined together constantly in prayer." In the King James Bible, this is expressed as, "These all continued with one accord in prayer." The thought expressed here is that they were in unity. Review the definition for *unity* in your Webster's 1828 *Dictionary*.

The power of the Holy Spirit enables us to communicate the Gospel and establish churches.

Unity with Diversity

### Discussion and Notebook Work

1. Record the memory verse and file.

   "Though I speak with the tongues of men and of angels, and have not charity [love], I am become as sounding brass, or a tinkling cymbal. And though I have the gift of prophecy, and understand all mysteries, and all knowledge; and though I have all faith, so that I could remove mountains, and have not charity, I am nothing." (1 Corinthians 13:1–2)

2. Practice the memory verses to recite at the end of the week.

3. Use your Bible dictionary-concordance to record the definitions for *lot* and *unity*. Read the related Scriptures.

4. Begin a **timeline** starting with the crucifixion and record the events of the New Testament church.

#### The New Testament Church Timeline

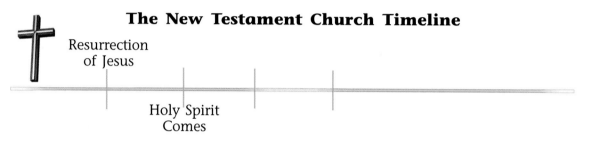

Resurrection of Jesus

Holy Spirit Comes

5. Use the **reciprocal teaching strategy** to study the Scriptures telling of instances when Jesus was seen after He was crucified on the cross:

   a. Mark 16:12, 14
   b. Luke 24:33–36
   c. John 20:19, 26
   d. John 21:1–14

6. Use the information you learned from the Scriptures above to explain why these accounts are reliable evidence that Jesus is alive.

7. Write a paragraph relating what Jesus' resurrection means to you.

*Enrichment activity*—Write a paragraph telling why you think unity was important for the disciples as they waited for the Holy Spirit. (Hint: This is a governmental principle you learned in history class.)

# The Coming of the Holy Spirit
## Acts 2

The Holy Spirit came upon the disciples on the day of Pentecost according to Acts 2:1–4. *Pentecost* was a special feast day celebrated by the Jews to thank God for the harvest of their crops. It was held fifty days after another special feast day they celebrated, the Passover. You may remember the first Passover was in Egypt before Moses led the people out of slavery. Jesus had been crucified on Passover and ascended forty days later. Ten days after

God uses the relationships in our lives to further the Gospel message.

that the Holy Spirit was poured out on the disciples gathered together in the upper room. They were given the power to witness, telling everything they had seen about Jesus.

Because of Pentecost, Jews from many other nations had gathered in Jerusalem to celebrate the feast. When the disciples spoke in languages they had never learned, the people from other nations each heard the Gospel in their own language. According to the Scriptures, three thousand people came to know God that day. These new converts spread the Gospel as they went back to their nations.

Besides speaking in different tongues, the believers showed their love for God and each other in other special ways. Read Acts 2:42–47 to identify the things the new church members did.

### Discussion and Notebook Work

1. Use your Bible dictionary-concordance to read the definitions for *Pentecost* and *tongue*. Read the related Scriptures.

2. Use a **concept/definition map** to define *witness*.

3. Read Peter's address to the crowd in Acts 2:14–41. Identify and record how Peter was able to convince the people that Jesus is the Christ (or *Messiah*) the Jews had been expecting to come.

4. From the reading of Acts 2:42–47, record the Scriptures and identify the special ways the new church members showed their love on a page like the one below. (See the examples.)

### Fellowship of Believers

| Scripture Verses from Acts 2:42–47 | Signs of Love |
|---|---|
| v. 42 *"They devoted themselves to the apostles' teaching and to the fellowship, to the breaking of bread and to prayer."* | • *Devoted to the apostles' teaching*<br>•<br>•<br>• |
| v. 44 | • |
| v. 46 | • *Broke bread and ate together* |
| v. 47 | • |

5. Write a paragraph relating how you can be a witness and how you can show Christian love.

6. Add to the New Testament church **timeline.**

# Healing Comes in the Name of Jesus
## Acts 3

In Acts chapter two, you learned how Peter preached boldly to the crowd and thousands came to know their Savior. This is certainly a different Peter than we saw just before Jesus was crucified. Not only did the power of the Holy Spirit enable him to speak boldly, but in Acts chapter three we see the power to heal released as he spoke to the crippled man in the name of Jesus Christ of Nazareth. The people who saw this miracle were amazed.

This miracle provided another opportunity for Peter to preach to the people about Jesus and how they could be forgiven of their sins. He must have preached a pretty convincing and convicting message because Acts 4:4 records that, "Many who heard the message believed, and the number of men grew to about five thousand."

Read Acts chapter three to learn how God healed the crippled beggar through Peter and how Peter spoke to the onlookers.

The power of the Holy Spirit enables us to communicate the Gospel and to establish churches.

### *Discussion and Notebook Work*

1. Discuss *providence* and *providential* and how God's providence is evident in the healing of the crippled man.

2. From the reading of Acts 3:11–26, find and summarize at least four things indicating how Peter explained God's providential preparation of Jesus to be the Savior.

3. Identify the three ways Peter addressed the onlookers and record your findings in a sentence or paragraph.

4. Add to the New Testament church **timeline.**

# Peter and John Face Opposition
## Acts 4

The power
of the
Holy Spirit
enables us to
communicate
the Gospel
and to
establish
churches.

Y ou learned previously about the crippled man who was healed when Peter told him to rise up and walk in the name of Jesus Christ of Nazareth. Many received Christ as their Savior because of this miracle.

There were those however, who were not at all happy about Peter's preaching. The priests, the captain of the temple, and the Sadducees confronted Peter and John. The Sadducees in particular were not happy with the preaching of the resurrection of the dead through Jesus. The Sadducees were a Jewish religious group that did not believe in the resurrection of the dead. They had Peter and John put in jail until the next morning when the important authorities were gathered together to decide what should be done with them.

Think about the courage it must have taken Peter and John to speak about Jesus in front of these powerful people and then how they might have felt when they were put in jail. These were the same people who plotted to have Jesus crucified. We are blessed to live in a nation where we have the freedom to speak publicly about what we believe. In some nations of the world, you can be killed simply for becoming a Christian. Even in our country, it is not always popular to tell people the truth about what the Bible says. We know the Bible is God's Word and it is true, but those who don't believe in God will fight against you for taking a stand that does not condone their sin.

In the end, the officials decided to release Peter and John with the warning "not to speak or teach at all in the name of Jesus." Read Acts 4:19–31 to learn how Peter and John responded to them and what they did when they were released.

### Discussion and Notebook Work

1. Use your Bible dictionary-concordance to compare and contrast the Sadducees and Pharisees using a **Venn diagram.**

2. Record and answer the reason questions.
   - How do you know Peter and John did not plan to stop preaching about Jesus?
   - What did they ask God for in prayer?
   - Do you think the disciples were more concerned for their safety or for preaching boldly? Explain.

3. Relate what you learned about prayer in Acts chapter four. Also, read the special feature, "Let's Live It: Power through Prayer."

4. Add to the New Testament church **timeline.**

# Those Who Serve God Will Suffer Persecution
## Acts 5

Those who follow Christ must be willing to suffer if necessary in order to bring God glory. Jesus said in Matthew 16:24–25, "If anyone would come after me, he must deny himself and take up his cross and follow me. For whoever wants to save his life will lose it, but whoever loses his life for me will find it." These verses mean that we must be willing to follow Jesus and obey Him no matter the cost to us personally.

We learned in last week's reading that Peter and John were briefly thrown in jail. You will learn today that the apostles did not stop preaching and teaching in the name of Jesus. They were fully committed to obeying God. As they preached, God answered their prayers for boldness, the healing of people, and the performing of signs and wonders in the name of Jesus. More and more people came to believe in the Lord Jesus Christ and brought their sick and those possessed by demon spirits to be healed.

The success of the apostles attracted the attention of the religious leaders who "were filled with jealousy." Peter and John were thrown in jail once again, but the outcome was more severe and nearly fatal this time. Read this account in Acts 5:17–42.

*Christian character is formed through suffering difficulties.*

### Discussion and Notebook Work

1. Record the memory verses, 1 Corinthians 13:3–4, underneath 1 Corinthians 13:1–2 and file.

   "And though I bestow all my goods to feed the poor, and though I give my body to be burned, and have not charity, it profiteth me nothing. Charity suffereth long, and is kind; charity envieth not; charity vaunteth not itself, is not puffed up." (1 Corinthians 13:3–4)

2. Practice the entire passage to recite at the end of the week.

3. Use your Bible dictionary-concordance to read the definitions for *Sanhedrin*, *flog*, and *persecution*. Read the related Scripture verses.

4. From Acts 5:17–42 record God's providence in sparing the lives of the apostles.

5. Identify and record a summary of the key events that happened to the apostles in Acts 5:17–42 on a **sequence chain.**

6. Relate a time you were rejected or challenged for your faith.

*Enrichment activity*—Participate in a **Readers Theatre activity** of events in Acts chapter five.

# Persecution Causes the Spread of the Gospel
## Acts 8

Opposition continued to grow as the number of people receiving the Gospel increased in Jerusalem. Then a disciple named Stephen was stoned for preaching the truth. Acts 8:1 says that, "On that day a great persecution broke out against the church at Jerusalem, and all except the apostles were scattered throughout Judea and Samaria." It's hard to imagine that persecution of the church could be a part of God's plan to spread the Gospel, but that is what happened. God can use a bad situation for good.

The Gospel spread into the region of Samaria. Read the definition for *Samaritan* in your Bible dictionary-concordance to learn about the Samaritan people. Simon the sorcerer came to Christ through the ministry of Philip in Samaria. Read the account of Simon the sorcerer found in Acts 8:9–25. Even though he had become a Christian, there were still character issues in his life that needed to be corrected. It's like the bumper sticker says, "Christians aren't perfect, just forgiven." We all have areas of our lives that need God's light to shine on them to expose the darkness of sin so we can ask God's forgiveness and repent.

### Discussion and Notebook Work

1. Use your Bible dictionary-concordance to record the definitions for *Samaritan* and *sorcery*. Read the related Scriptures.

2. Use a **T-chart** to record the character of Simon the sorcerer before and after he became a Christian.

3. Relate in a paragraph how your character is being changed because of knowing Jesus.

4. Add to the New Testament church **timeline.**

# God's Grace Falls upon Saul
## Acts 9

When Stephen was being stoned, we read that a young man named Saul approved or consented to his death. This is the first time the Bible mentions Saul, who was about to have his life completely changed. Romans 2:4b says, "God's kindness leads you toward repentance." In the King James Bible, this portion of Scripture is translated, "The goodness of God leadeth thee to repentance." God knew Saul's character, his family, his education, even how zealous and dedicated he was in the practice of his religion. Saul thought he was living a life pleasing to God even while he was persecuting and killing Christians. God chose him to carry the Gospel to the Gentiles, the people who were not Jews. Acts 9:16 also says, "I will show him how much he must suffer for my name." As you learn more about Saul's life, you will learn how true this statement is. God never guaranteed that the things we are called to do in life would be easy, but God says He will always be with us in them and give us the grace to obey Him in everything. Read about Saul's conversion in Acts 9:1–31.

The apostles were willing to suffer to bring the Gospel to others.

### Discussion and Notebook Work

1. Use your Bible dictionary-concordance to record the definitions for *Gentile* and *convert*. Read the related Scriptures.

2. Record and answer the reason questions:

   a. How do we know that Saul's reputation was known far and wide?

   b. Not all the people believed Saul had become a Christian. How did people respond to the news of his conversion?

   c. How did Christians show Saul love and acceptance after his conversion?

3. Complete a **T-chart** about Paul before and after conversion using Acts chapter nine.

Paul—Before and After Conversion

| Saul—The Persecutor | Paul—The Preacher |
|---|---|
| | |

4. Begin a **"People Who Impacted History" chart** for Paul.

5. Add to the New Testament church **timeline**.

# The Gospel Is for All Men
## Acts 10

Difficulties form Christian character.

Do you know the story of Peter's vision of the sheet being let down from heaven with all kinds of animals on it? Peter was hungry, so God told him to kill and eat of them. This shocked Peter because the Old Testament law taught Jews not to eat certain animals that God had called unclean. God was trying to communicate a truth to Peter. While Peter was thinking about the meaning of the vision, men arrived to bring him to a Roman centurion named Cornelius. Peter obeyed the voice of the Spirit of God and went with the men.

The Scriptures don't say exactly when Peter realized the meaning of the vision. It could be that as the circumstances occurred the meaning of the vision became clear. Learning to interpret the meaning of what God says to us often takes time. Sometimes God will speak to us through His Word a truth that applies to our need or situation. He will help us understand His message to us when we need it. Eventually God made the meaning clear to Peter. Read Acts chapter ten.

130　　　　　　**New Testament History**

### Discussion and Notebook Work

1. Use your Bible dictionary-concordance to record the definition for *vision*. Read the related Scriptures.

2. Complete a **story map** for Acts chapter ten.

3. Draw a picture with your colored pencils representing the portion of Scripture about Peter's vision.

4. Relate how you can witness to people who are different than you.

5. Add these events to the New Testament church **timeline.**

# A Time of Preparation for Paul
## Acts 11; Galatians 2

The focus of our lesson this class is Saul, a man who had a great influence on New Testament history. This man had been a persecutor of Christians. You have learned that many Christians were unsure whether his conversion was real. Jews did not want him preaching about Jesus and tried to have him killed. The disciples helped him to escape their plot and eventually sent him to his home in Tarsus for protection. There is a period of fourteen years that Paul seemed to be hidden away as God prepared and brought revelation to him. Galatians 2:1–10 tells us that the next time he went to Jerusalem was fourteen years later. At this time, he communicated with the leaders of the church about his ministry to the Gentiles. They approved of him and believed God had ordained him for this ministry.

Read Acts 11:19–30 to see the beginning of Paul's ministry in Antioch.

> Church government is appointed by God.

### Discussion and Notebook Work

1. Record the memory verses, 1 Corinthians 13:5–6, underneath 1 Corinthians 13:3–4 and file.

    "Doth not behave itself unseemly, seeketh not her own, is not easily provoked, thinketh no evil; Rejoiceth not in iniquity, but rejoiceth in the truth." (1 Corinthians 13:5–6)

2. Practice the entire passage to recite at the end of the week.

3. Use Webster's 1828 *Dictionary* and your Bible dictionary-concordance to complete a **concept/definition map** for *revelation*.

4. Record and answer the reason questions.

  a. How do you see church government working in Acts chapter eleven?
  b. Why did Barnabas go to find Paul?
  c. How can you tell that the people of the church had begun to trust in Paul's conversion and trustworthiness?

5. Continue adding to your **"People Who Impacted History" chart** for Paul.

6. Add to the New Testament church **timeline.**

*Enrichment activity*—Read the account from Paul himself of God confirming his ministry to the Gentiles in Galatians 2:1–10.

# Paul's First Missionary Journey
## Acts 13

Church government is appointed by God.

In Antioch, the Holy Spirit told the leaders of the church that Barnabas and Saul were to be sent out as missionaries. Their path was directed by the Holy Spirit. In Acts chapter thirteen, we begin to see Saul stepping into his God-ordained role as a leader and teacher. We also see Saul operating in the gifts of the Holy Spirit in dealing with the Jewish sorcerer and in standing up to teach. Jesus said in Mark 16:17 that signs would follow them that believe. Mark 16:20 says, "Then the disciples went out and preached everywhere, and the Lord worked with them and confirmed his word by the signs that accompanied it." Read Acts 13:1–26 to see how God anointed Saul to minister and to learn when he began to be known as Paul.

### Discussion and Notebook Work

1. Use your Bible dictionary-concordance to read the definition for *synagogue*. Read the related Scriptures.

2. Record and answer the reason questions.

  a. How did the church at Antioch receive their direction for Barnabas and Saul?
  b. How can you tell that Paul was an educated and knowledgeable man?

3. Read Acts 13:27–52 to record the Old Testament Scriptures Paul used to identify Jesus as the Savior of both Jews and Gentiles.

4. Complete a **sequence chain** of the key events of Paul's missionary trip in Acts chapter thirteen.

5. Continue to add to the **"People Who Impacted History" chart** for Paul.

6. Add to the New Testament church **timeline.**

*Enrichment activity*—Record the reason questions and relate how you can respond to missionaries who visit your church:

a. How can you be helped by their teaching and by hearing about their experiences?

b. How can you be helpful to these missionaries?

The Work of the Apostles

# Good Soldiers of Jesus Christ Endure Hardship
## Acts 14

Later in Paul's ministry, he instructed a son in the faith named Timothy to "endure hardship with us like a good soldier of Christ Jesus." Paul knew a lot about hardships. In 2 Corinthians 11:25 he says, "Three times I was beaten with rods, once I was stoned, three times I was shipwrecked, I spent a night and a day in the open sea." The list of Paul's trials goes on. Paul discovered the difficulty of preaching to people who were different that he was. Not only were there language barriers, but there were differences in

Paul and Barnabas were led by the Holy Spirit in determining what to teach.

their cultures. The people Paul met on his missionary journeys worshipped different gods and had different social traditions. Paul and Barnabas also learned that they could be very popular one minute and very hated the next. Read Acts 14:8–20 to learn of the difficulties Paul and Barnabas faced.

### Discussion and Notebook Work

1. Record and answer the reason questions.

   a. Why were Paul and Barnabas so upset that the crowds wanted to offer sacrifices to them?

   b. Are there those today who would gladly accept the honors the people wanted to give Paul and Barnabas? Explain.

2. Participate in a **Readers Theatre activity** for Acts chapter fourteen.

3. Add to the **"People Who Impacted History" chart.**

# Church Government in Action
## Acts 15

Church government is appointed by God and brings safety and counsel.

When two or more people are together, there are always opportunities for disagreements. How do you solve disagreements with your brothers and sisters, friends, or classmates? Do you try to solve the problem on your own or with God's help through prayer? Or do you go to your parents or your teacher for help in resolving conflicts? Sometimes it's necessary to go to a higher authority when things don't seem to be working out. That's why every organization has leaders who examine the difficult issues and seek solutions to disagreements and problems. In the New Testament church, the apostles and elders in Jerusalem made up the council that solved disputes. Because they knew God's Word, were recognized as having been with Jesus, and were men of prayer, their decisions were generally accepted by the New Testament churches. Read Acts 15:1–21 to see what the problem was that needed to be resolved.

### Discussion and Notebook Work

1. Write a paragraph summarizing the problem which the apostles and elders in Jerusalem needed to solve.

2. Read and discuss Acts 15:22–35 to learn the process the council in Jerusalem chose to solve the problem.

3. Use the letter in Acts 15 as a model and write a letter communicating the rules for Gentile believers to follow.

4. Continue to add to the **"People Who Impacted History" chart** for Paul.

# A Parting of Ways
## Acts 15, 16

In your Bible, Amos 3:3 says, "Do two walk together unless they have agreed to do so?" The Kings James Version translates the verse this way, "Can two walk together, except they be agreed?" Guess what? Even the best of people can disagree at times on the way to accomplish common goals. That's what happened to Paul and Barnabas. After working well together for so long, they disagreed on whether they should take John Mark with them on their second missionary trip. Barnabas was John Mark's uncle and wanted to give him another chance even John Mark had dropped out on their first trip. The conflict caused a parting of ways. Paul chose Silas to go with him. Along the way a young disciple named Timothy also joined Paul and Silas. In the long run, it was a good thing because there were now two missionary teams carrying the Gospel.

The Holy Spirit continued to direct the missionary effort. Paul had a vision of where to go next. It just so happened that as they went outside the city of Philippi along the river to pray, they met several women there and began

The Chain of Christianity® moves westward.

New Testament History                                                      135 to talk to them. Lydia, an influential woman among them, and her whole household were baptized. She then opened her house to the missionaries. Can you see God's hand in this? Some things that we think of as coincidental are really God's providence. Read Acts 15:36–16:15.

### *Discussion and Notebook Work*

1. Record the memory verses, 1 Corinthians 13:7–8, underneath 1 Corinthians 13:5–6 and file.

   "Beareth all things, believeth all things, hopeth all things, endureth all things. Charity never faileth: but whether there be prophecies, they shall fail; whether there be tongues, they shall cease; whether there be knowledge, it shall vanish away." (1 Corinthians 13:7–8)

2. Practice the entire passage to recite at the end of the week.

3. Draw and color one of the scenes you just read.

4. Record and answer the reason questions.

   a. What was the good result from the split between Barnabas and Paul?
   b. Tell why Paul chose Timothy to travel with him and what message they preached.
   c. Tell how God directed Paul to Macedonia and what this teaches about obeying God.
   d. How was Lydia changed by Paul's preaching and who brought about the change in her?

5. Tell of a time when you resolved a conflict with a friend God's way.

6. Continue to add to the **"People Who Impacted History" chart** for Paul.

7. Add to the New Testament church **timeline.**

# The Power of Praise
## Acts 16

The Word of God teaches us that the tongue is a powerful thing that can be used for good or evil. Proverbs 18:21a says, "The tongue has the power of life and death." Acts 16:16–40 tells the story of how Paul

**New Testament History**

and Silas found themselves in prison. You would think after being stripped and beaten, the disciples would be pretty unhappy. Not so with Paul and Silas! The Scripture records that they were singing and praying to God at midnight. There is a lesson to be learned here. In the Kings James Version of the Bible, Psalms 22:3 tells us that God inhabits the praises of His people, and when God shows up, look out—He comes with His power! Sometimes we get into the bad habit of complaining about every hard thing that happens to us. God wants us to speak words of faith and hope rather than murmuring words of doubt, unbelief, and grumbling.

Read Acts 16:16–40 to discover how the power of praise turned a bad situation into a victorious one.

### Discussion and Notebook Work

1. Use your Bible dictionary-concordance to record the definition for *praise*. Read the related Scriptures.

2. Complete a **story map** to record the events that happened to Paul and Silas in prison.

3. Think of a situation in your own life where you need to speak more positively. Describe this in a paragraph.

4. Add to the **"People Who Impacted History" chart**.

5. Add to the New Testament church **timeline**.

# Paul Ministers in Athens, Greece
## Acts 16–17

When the missionaries arrived in a new city, they would first go to the Jewish synagogues where Paul would reason with the citizens from the Scriptures. Perhaps Gentile believers would also be present to hear the readings from the Old Testament. You see, Paul was an educated man. His writings record how God prepared him for ministry. In Acts 22:3 he tells of being born a Jew in Tarsus and educated by Gamaliel, who was a respected teacher and Pharisee. In verses 25–28 of the same chapter, he reveals his Roman citizenship. In Acts 23:6, we learn that he was a Pharisee and the son of a Pharisee. These things and his fourteen years of preparation after he was saved came together to equip him for his evangelistic ministry. This is God's providential hand at work in Paul's life.

You will learn of Paul's skill in relating to his audience as you read about his ministry to the Jews and Greeks in Athens. He was able to reason with them because he knew Scripture so well and was familiar with their interest in new ideas and religion. He also was well trained in presenting information to his listeners so as to persuade them to believe in the Gospel message. As you read Acts 17:16–34, look for how he was able to establish a link to this audience. However, even if you are well trained, the Holy Spirit has to prepare a person's heart to receive Christ as Savior, and only God can save.

### Discussion and Notebook Work

1. Record and answer the reason questions.
   a. What topic did Paul begin talking about to the men of Athens beginning in Acts 17:22–23 in order to connect with them?
   b. How did Paul confront their worship of idols?
   c. Do you think Paul was concerned that he might offend the people with his message? Explain why or why not.

2. Skim Acts 17 to compare the success of the ministry to the different people groups Paul and Silas visited. Create and complete a page similar to the following example.

**New Testament History**

| City | Persecution or Not | Success of Ministry | Topic(s) of Teaching |
|------|--------------------|--------------------|----------------------|
| Thessalonica | | | |
| Berea | | | |
| Athens | | | |

3. Add to the **"People Who Impacted History" chart.**

4. Add to the New Testament church **timeline.**

*Enrichment activity*—Participate in a **Readers Theatre activity** of Paul's preaching in Acts 17:24–31.

# A Familiar Pattern
## Acts 18

The Chain of Christianity® moves westward.

As you learned from reading Acts chapter seventeen, Paul had some success in Athens. However, there were many who resisted the message of the Gospel. Often Paul would find that the Jews were jealous and they would cause the most trouble for him. In Acts chapter eighteen, we find Paul ministering in Corinth, where he finally became fed up with opposition from the Jews. James 3:16 says, "For where you have envy and selfish ambition, there you find disorder and every evil practice."

Read Acts 18:1–22 to learn what kind of opposition faced Paul this time and how he handled it.

### Discussion and Notebook Work

1. Record and answer the reason questions.
   a. From the reading about Paul's ministry, why did some of the Jews become jealous or envious of him?
   b. In Acts 18:9–11, God spoke to Paul in a vision. Why do you think God said what He did?
   c. What kind of effect did the vision have on Paul? Explain your answer.
2. Write a paragraph explaining how you see God's providential hand in Paul's ministry.

   ⋆ Include examples of the actions Jews took against Paul.
   ⋆ Tell how Paul reacted to their opposition.
3. Relate how one should respond when a friend rejects the Good News of Jesus.
4. Add to the **"People Who Impacted History" chart** for Paul.

# Paul's Third Missionary Journey
## Acts 19; Deuteronomy 18

The Chain of Christianity® moves westward.

Paul's third missionary journey is introduced in Acts 18:23. His purpose in traveling place to place through Galatia and Phrygia was to encourage the new Christians. This was important to help protect the new disciples from falling away or receiving false teaching. We see new disciples mentioned who supported Paul and others who were called to the ministry like Paul. However, we learn in Acts chapter nineteen that some people tried to minister in the name of Jesus without actually knowing Jesus. This is a dangerous thing because the power to set people free from sin or demons comes only from Jesus Christ. The Lord gives this power to His disciples. There were consequences that came upon the people trying to minister without knowing Him.

Unlike those who tried to minister without knowing Jesus, Paul's ministry of God's Word in the city of Ephesus was confirmed with signs and wonders. Read Acts 19:1–22 to learn what happened when the Word was preached with God's power.

### Discussion and Notebook Work.

1. Record the memory verses, 1 Corinthians 13:9–10, underneath 1 Corinthians 13:7–8 and file.

   "For we know in part, and we prophesy in part. But when that which is perfect is come, then that which is in part shall be done away." (1 Corinthians 13:9–10)

2. Practice the entire passage the verses to recite at the end of the week.

3. Record the reason questions and answer them in complete sentences:
   a. How did the people demonstrate repentance of their occult activities?
   b. Name the occult practices in today's world that you must turn away from if you want to honor the Lord Jesus. Explain in a sentence or paragraph.

4. Many people in the city of Ephesus were involved in occult activities, which are forbidden by God. Read Deuteronomy 18:9–13 and tell what you learned.

5. Continue to add to the **"People Who Impacted History" chart** for Paul.

6. Add to the New Testament church **timeline.**

# Resistance Comes against "the Way"
## Acts 19–20

Persecution spread the Gospel message.

In Acts 19:9 it says that, "But some of them [the Jews] became obstinate; they refused to believe and publicly maligned the Way." This is the first use of the term referring to Christians. It is mentioned again in verse 23. Use your Webster's 1828 *Dictionary* to learn the definitions for *obstinate* and *maligned*.

Not only did some Jews come against Paul and his disciples, but the Ephesians who worshipped idols came against them as well. The motives for each of the groups to resist the truth were different. Acts 19:29 says, "Soon the whole city was in an uproar." You may have seen images in books, newspapers or even on TV where people are behaving badly without self-control. Words like *chaos, anarchy,* and *riot* are used to describe these situations. Even though God had protected Paul in turbulent times before, he listened to wise counsel and did not appear before these stirred-up crowds. It's important to listen to wise counsel. If Paul had been proud or stubborn, he could have lost his life. Paul had to leave the city after things calmed down.

### Discussion and Notebook Work

1. Use Webster's 1828 *Dictionary* to record the definitions for *obstinate* and *malign.*

2. Use your Bible dictionary-concordance to define *way* and read the related Scriptures.

3. Discuss the use of the word *Way* in Acts 19:9 and 19:23.

4. The Jews and Ephesians both resisted Paul. Compare their motives.

5. Participate in a **Readers Theatre activity** of the events described in Acts 19:23–20:1.

6. Add to the New Testament church **timeline.**

# Finish the Race and Complete the Task
## Acts 20

You are going to read a sad chapter in Paul's life. He is being led by the Holy Spirit back to Jerusalem. There have been words of prophecy that prison and suffering are in his future. So he is saying goodbye to his friends and fellow disciples, knowing he will never see them again. He must have felt some uneasiness about the future and great sadness at the closing of a chapter in his life.

The apostles were willing to suffer to bring the Gospel to others.

Paul mentions a phrase while communicating his farewell to the elders of the Ephesian church that summarized the goal of his life's work: "If only I may finish the race and complete the task the Lord Jesus has given me—the task of testifying to the Gospel of God's grace." (Acts 20:24) Paul also mentioned this race in 1 Corinthians 9:24–27. Paul speaks of the training required to run in a race. Perhaps you know something about this—to compete for a prize requires discipline and endurance. Your race may require courage to face your fears and step out into the unknown trusting God to meet you and help you overcome your difficulties. Read Acts 20:13–36 and see if you can relate to how Paul was feeling. Read Acts 21 to discover what happened to Paul.

### Discussion and Notebook Work

1. Use your Bible dictionary-concordance to record the definition for *succeed*.
2. Compare Paul's standard of success and the world's view of success.

#### Views of Success

| Paul's View of Success | World's View of Success |
| --- | --- |
| | |

3. Write a paragraph telling about a time in your life that was similar to Paul leaving his friends.
4. Continue to add to the **"People Who Impacted History" chart.**
5. Add to the New Testament church **timeline.**

*Enrichment activity*—Paraphrase a section of Paul's farewell address in Acts 20:18–36.

# Prophesy Is Fulfilled in Paul's Life
## Acts 21

The Chain of Christianity® moved westward as persecution caused the Gospel message to be carried to other parts of the world.

As you learned in Acts chapter twenty, there was prophecy of the hardship and imprisonment to come in Paul's life. As he went on his way to Jerusalem, further warnings came confirming the earlier messages. A prophesy was acted out by the prophet Agabus. By binding his own hands and feet with Paul's belt, Agabus showed how Paul would be treated in Jerusalem. The disciples tried to persuade him not to go, but as you read before, Paul felt compelled by the Holy Spirit to go to Jerusalem regardless of the suffering it would mean for him. Read the definition of *compel* in Webster's 1828 *Dictionary* to better understand this word.

When Paul reached Jerusalem, the prophecies came to pass (as they always do when they are truly of God). Paul was taken before the ruling Roman officials with charges by the Jewish religious leaders. The religious leaders wanted to kill Paul just like they wanted to kill Jesus. In serving Jesus, his Savior, Paul was willing to suffer beatings, rejection, and humiliation to fulfill God's purpose in his life. Jesus laid down his life to pay for our sins so that we might receive eternal life. Paul was willing to lay down his life to carry the message of the Gospel wherever God led him.

Read Acts 21:17–36 to discover the order of events that brought about Paul's imprisonment.

### Discussion and Notebook Work

1. Use your Bible dictionary-concordance to record the definition for *prophecy*. Read the related Scriptures.

2. Use a **sequence chain** to record the events that brought about Paul's imprisonment.

3. Record and answer the reason questions.
   a. Why did Paul ignore the warnings of the prophet and his friends?
   b. What did Paul do in order not to offend the Jerusalem church?
   c. Why was Paul arrested?

4. Think about the choices you make. What compels you in making your choices? (Ask yourself, "Who or what is in control?")

   For example: How do you respond when your parents ask you:
   * To do household chores
   * To do your homework
   * To help a neighbor or family member

5. Add to the New Testament church **timeline.**

# Paul Courageously Stands for Jesus
## Acts 23

You will learn in Acts chapter twenty-three that Paul, like Jesus, was also put on trial and taken before the chief priests. He was not afraid of them and spoke boldly and confidently, "My brothers, I have fulfilled my duty to God in all good conscience to this day." You may remember what the Lord said to Ananias about Paul's conversion in Acts 9:16, "I will show him how much he must suffer for my name." Verse two says the high priest ordered someone to strike him on the mouth. Nevertheless Paul maintained his composure and spoke with wisdom. In that moment, God gave Paul the words to speak. Jesus taught His disciples this very thing recorded in Luke 12:11–12,

God has a plan for each person's life.

"When you are brought before synagogues, rulers and authorities, do not worry about how you will defend yourselves or what you will say, for the Holy Spirit will teach you at that time what you should say."

Because Paul said that he was a Pharisee on trial for believing in the resurrection of the dead, a division developed that ultimately helped Paul to be delivered from their hands. God brought comfort and revelation to Paul that night about His plan for him. Men may rebel against God's plans, but He is Sovereign. It will be just as the Lord's prayer in Matthew 6:10 says, "your kingdom come, your will be done on earth as it is in heaven." Read of these things in Acts 23:1–11.

### *Discussion and Notebook Work*

1. Record the memory verses, 1 Corinthians 13:11–12, underneath 1 Corinthians 13:9–10 and file.

   "When I was a child, I spake as a child, I understood as a child, I thought as a child: but when I became a man, I put away childish things. For now we see through a glass, darkly; but then face to face: now I know in part; but then shall I know even as also I am known." (1 Corinthians 13:11–12)

2. Practice the entire passage to recite at the end of the week.

3. Use your Bible dictionary-concordance to record the definition for *Sanhedrin*. Read the related Scripture.

4. Record and answer the reason questions.

   a. How was Paul able to divide the assembly of Pharisees and Sadducees?
   b. How did the plot against Paul fail? Who did God use to help Paul?

5. Participate in a **Readers Theatre activity** of Paul's appearance before the Sanhedrin.

6. Continue the **"People Who Impacted History" chart** for Paul.

New Testament History

# Paul's Last Missionary Journey Begins
## Acts 24

Through all that happened to Paul, the Scriptures record his faithfulness to present the message of the Gospel regardless of the consequences. Because of the accusations of the Jews, Paul was taken to Caesarea to appear before the Roman governor Felix. A case was presented against him, but once again Paul persuasively defended himself. Felix did not rule on the case right away, but after several days he called for Paul to come and discuss faith in Christ with him and his Jewish wife. Felix sent for Paul to speak with him frequently; considering the boldness God had given Paul, surely they often talked about the grace of Jesus Christ. Felix held Paul in prison for two years until the next governor came to power. Scripture does not record whether Felix ever accepted Jesus as his Savior. Read about Felix's response to Paul's defense in Acts 24:22–27.

God has a plan for each person's life.

### Discussion and Notebook Work

1. Review and discuss the definition for *grace*.

2. Relate a time you were aware of the grace of Jesus Christ in your life.

3. Reread Acts 24:25. Explain why Felix became afraid and tell why you think he did not respond to Paul's preaching.

5. Reread the trial found in Acts 24:1–21. Record on a **T-chart** Tertullus's accusations and how Paul responded to them.

5. Add to the New Testament church **timeline.**

# God's Providential Plan for Paul
## Acts 25

Remember, Paul has been in prison for two years now with no evidence that would convict him of a crime. However, God's ways are not our ways, and God provided Paul with the grace to love Him, trust Him, and obey Him, even in prison without cause. In Acts 23:11 God told Paul, "Take courage! As you have testified about me in Jerusalem, so you must also testify in Rome." Just as God had said, the Scriptures record in Acts chapter twenty-five that Paul's next trial was before Festus, the new Roman governor.

Every step of the way, God providentially watched over Paul and enabled him to fulfill his God-given purpose. God preserved Paul from another plot to take his life. When Festus asked Paul if he was willing to go to Jerusalem to answer the charges, Paul appealed to Caesar. As a Roman citizen, Paul had the right to be tried in a Roman court and appealing to Caesar meant that he would be sent to Rome for that purpose. Paul would receive his request, but not before giving his testimony before Festus and King Agrippa.

There is a song by Gary Paxton that encourages us to ask ourselves, "If you were on trial for being a Christian, would there be enough evidence to convict you?"[1] The evidence is clear for Paul's life. What about yours?

### Discussion and Notebook Work

1. Write a paragraph relating how your life shows other people evidence of your relationship with Christ.

2. Review Acts 24 and read Acts 25 to answer the following: What providential role did Felix and Festus play in seeing that Paul was sent to Rome?

*Our lives give testimony to God's providence.*

# Paul Evangelizes Roman and Jewish Leaders
## Acts 26

**L**ook in your Webster's 1828 *Dictionary* to read the definitions for *testify* and *testimony*. You have probably never had to testify in a court of law under oath to the following, "Do you solemnly swear to tell the truth, the whole truth, and nothing but the truth, so help you God?" The testimony of Paul before Festus and King Agrippa was the truth about his life. It also was the truth about how he came to know Jesus of Nazareth as his Savior. Christians need to be able to tell their story (how they came to know Christ) to other believers and unbelievers in order to show the power of God to change a life. Read Paul's testimony in Acts 26:1–23.

### Discussion and Notebook Work

1. Use your Bible dictionary-concordance to record the definition for *testimony*.

2. From the reading of Acts chapter twenty-six, identify the important points that might persuade an unbeliever to become a Christian.

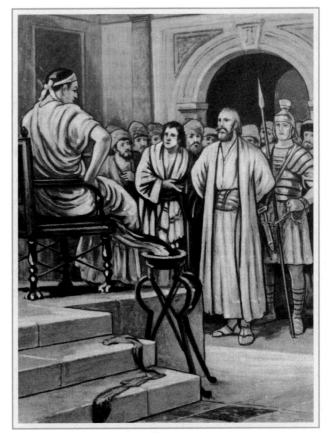

3. Write the testimony of how you came to know Jesus as your Savior (if applicable).

4. Continue to add to the **"People Who Impacted History" chart.**

# The Letter of First Corinthians
## 1 Corinthians 3

The Corinthian church was birthed during Paul's first missionary trip to Corinth. It was a church consisting mainly of Gentiles with no knowledge of the Old Testament or the religious traditions of the Jews. Though they had received Christ by faith, they were still learning how to live out their Christianity. The culture in which they lived was very immoral and wicked. The Corinthians were having trouble separating themselves from the sin and pagan influences of the culture in which they lived. In other words, their lives were a mixture of the two worlds. There was a need for further instruction so that these baby Christians could grow up and become spiritually mature.

Have you ever felt torn between what God wants you to be and do and what others (maybe even you) want you to be? Read 1 Corinthians chapter three to see what Paul had to say to the Corinthians.

### Discussion and Notebook Work

1. Record the memory verse, 1 Corinthians 13:13, underneath 1 Corinthians 13:11–12 and file.

   "And now abideth faith, hope, charity, these three; but the greatest of these is charity." (1 Corinthians 13:13)

2. Practice the entire passage to recite at the end of the week.

3. Use Webster's 1828 *Dictionary* to record the definition for *division*.

4. Record and answer the reason questions.

   a. What were some behaviors that Paul said caused division in the Corinthian church?

   b. What do you think Paul means when he calls the Corinthians *worldly*?

   c. Are you influenced by the non-Christian environment of our nation? How?

# Paul Confronts the Sins of the Corinthian Church
## 1 Corinthians 8, 10

You read about the disputes that caused divisions in the Corinthian church. There were other serious moral issues affecting this church concerning marriage and sexual purity. In his letter, Paul corrects the church and instructs them in how to discipline believers who are sinning. The Corinthians were also divided over whether or not Christians should eat food first sacrificed to idols. In unit three, you researched the definition of *idol* and thought about the kind of things that might become an idol in your life. Take time to review the definition in your Bible dictionary-concordance. Now read 1 Corinthians chapter eight about food sacrificed to idols.

### Discussion and Notebook Work

1. Use your Bible dictionary-concordance to record the definition for *conscience*. Read the related Scriptures.

2. Summarize Paul's counsel regarding food sacrificed to idols.

3. Discuss how the Principle "Conscience Is the Most Sacred of All Property" applies to 1 Corinthians 8:9–13.

4. Read the discussion on eating continued in 1 Corinthians 10:23–33.

   ⋆ Discuss how this compares to what you read in 1 Corinthians chapter eight.

   ⋆ Reason how we can glorify God in our freedom.

Paul cultivated relationships with the churches through letters and visits.

Conscience Is the Most Sacred of All Property.

# Teaching on the Body of Christ
## 1 Corinthians 12

One of the more interesting teachings of Paul in this letter to the Corinthians is the use of metaphor in likening the church to a body. This is found in 1 Corinthians 12:12–31 and is subtitled *One Body, Many Parts* in your Bible. It emphasizes the importance of unity, oneness, or agreement. Review the definition for *unity* in your Webster's 1828 *Dictionary*. Read this portion of Scripture to identify the attitudes that are necessary for maintaining the unity of the spirit in any group.

### *Discussion and Notebook Work*

Record and answer the reason questions below:

1. What attitudes must you have toward other Christians in order to have unity in the body of Christ according to your reading?
2. Discuss the Principle, "Unity with Diversity."
3. Tell how Christians together are like a human body.
4. Why can't one Christian say he does not need another Christian?
5. Besides in the church, what other groups or activities are you aware of that require unity to be successful? Explain your answer.

Unity with Diversity

*Enrichment activity*—Draw a picture of the body parts talking to each other in 1 Corinthians chapter twelve.

# The Evidence of Resurrection to Eternal Life
## 1 Corinthians 15

Paul's teaching concludes in 1 Corinthians chapter fifteen with a discussion of the resurrection of Christ, the resurrection of the dead, and the resurrection of the body. It's important for every Christian to understand this doctrine as an essential part of the Gospel and be able to explain the evidence that supports it. Paul begins by reporting the evidence that Christ died for our sins and were raised from the dead. He explains that if Christ were not raised from the dead, then we have no hope ourselves of being raised from the dead to eternal life.

No other religion can give evidence that their god is alive. Christians know that our God is alive, that He still speaks today, and that He wants to have a relationship with us. The Bible is considered, even by non-Christian scholars, to be a very reliable ancient document. Read 1 Corinthians 15:1–20 to find the evidence that Christ is alive.

*Because God is relational, we need to cultivate Godly relationships.*

### Discussion and Notebook Work

1. Use your Bible dictionary-concordance to record the definition for *resurrection*. Read the related Scriptures.

2. Record the evidence given by Paul in a paragraph that proves our Savior and God is alive.

3. Read about the resurrection body in 1 Corinthians 15:35–58.

4. Use a **T-chart** to compare and contrast our earthly bodies and our resurrected bodies.

5. Relate an instance when God gave you victory over sin or a temptation such as selfishness, jealousy, anger, and fear.

# The Letter of Second Corinthians
## 2 Corinthians 10

This letter from Paul to the Corinthians does not teach as much doctrine as the letter of 1 Corinthians. However, it does reveal a lot to us about the sufferings, persecution, misunderstandings, and attacks Paul had to endure. He here defended his ministry.

Evidently, Paul was being criticized for how he spoke, his appearance, the content of his letters, and other things that had nothing to do with the truth of God's Word or his teaching of kingdom principles and right living. The criticisms probably had more to do with the Greek culture in which the Corinthians lived and what they believed to be proper.

Read 2 Corinthians chapter ten to see if you can identify the criticisms that Paul is addressing in his defense.

### Discussion and Notebook Work

1. Record the memory verses and file.

   The Great Commission
   "And Jesus came and spake unto them, saying, All power is given unto me in heaven and in earth. Go ye therefore, and teach all nations, baptizing them in the name of the Father, and of the Son, and of the Holy Ghost: Teaching them to observe all things whatsoever I have commanded you; and, lo, I am with you always, even unto the end of the world." (Matthew 28:18–20)

2. Practice the verses to recite at the end of next week.

3. Record the criticisms Paul was addressing in the defense of his ministry.
   * 2 Corinthians 10:1–6
   * 2 Corinthians 10:7–8
   * 2 Corinthians 10:12–13
   * 2 Corinthians 10:14–15

4. When you do a job, do you do it for the praise of men or for God's approval? What should your motivation be? Explain.

5. Complete the **"People Who Impacted History" chart.**

The Great Commission is for all Christians.

# Warning against Fellowship with Unbelievers
## 2 Corinthians 6, 7

The Great
Commission
is for all
Christians.

In your Bible, the subtitle of the portion of Scripture you will be reading is *Do Not Be Yoked With Unbelievers.* Look up the definition of *yoke* in the back of your Bible dictionary-concordance. Then read the definitions in your Webster's 1828 *Dictionary*. To be yoked together with someone is a close joining with the person. Paul's warning is not telling us to cut off all contact with unbelievers—otherwise, how could we take the Gospel to them? It's about carefully choosing the kind of companions or friends who will draw us closer to God instead of separating us from Him. Read Paul's advice in 2 Corinthians 6:14–7:1.

### Discussion and Notebook Work

1. Record a definition for *yoke* regarding relationships and use it in a sentence.

2. Write a paragraph telling how you can apply this passage to your relationships.

3. Read and record on a page similar to the one below Paul's advice regarding relationships in 1 Corinthians 5:9–10, 1 Corinthians 7:12–13, and 2 Corinthians 6:14–17.

### Christian Relationships

| 1 Corinthians 5:9–10 | 1 Corinthians 7:12–13 | 2 Corinthians 6:14–17 |
|---|---|---|
| | | |

4. Use the information from the chart on Christian relationships to write a summary statement about the relationships of a believer.

# The Law of Giving in God's Kingdom
## 2 Corinthians 8–9

Christians minister the Gospel in different ways.

Giving to God and to others is one of God's commands. Like all obedience, obeying God in this area releases a blessing on your life. Remember, God is a giver and He made us in His image. At some point, you have probably memorized John 3:16a, "For God so loved the world, that he gave his only begotten Son." Jesus taught the disciples in Luke 6:38 to, "Give, and it will be given to you. A good measure, pressed down, shaken together and running over, will be poured into your lap. For with the measure you use, it will be measured to you."

In chapters eight and nine, Paul speaks to the Corinthians about their giving to the needs of the saints and the blessings that come with the giving. Paul likens our giving to the farmer sowing seed. Read 2 Corinthians 9:6–15 for Paul's teaching on this matter.

### Discussion and Notebook Work

1. Complete a **vocabulary word analysis chart** for *generosity*.
2. Reread 2 Corinthians 9:10–11. People in our culture think of blessings as material goods. Can you see any other way God blesses people for their giving?
3. Explain how Paul's illustration of sowing seeds shows the benefits of giving.
4. Summarize Paul's advice on giving from 2 Corinthians 8:10–15.

# False Apostles
## 2 Corinthians 11

The Great
Commission
is for all
Christians.

I t was mentioned in a previous lesson that the church in Corinth was having trouble staying separate from the worldly ways of the culture in which they lived. In addition to this struggle there were those who preached a false Gospel, or taught things about God that weren't true. Because there were no mature leaders in their midst, who had a deep knowledge of the Word of God, the people were easily swayed to believe lies.

Paul addressed his concerns about false apostles in 2 Corinthians 11. God had prepared Paul through his education and extensive time alone with Him before beginning his ministry. He had the knowledge to answer their theological questions and to instruct them in righteous living. Nevertheless, Paul was required to fight for them like a shepherd must fight off the wolf from the flock of sheep.

Just like it was in Paul's day, there are many false teachers in our culture today who are capable of deceiving you if you don't know the truth. Your parents have been given the responsibility for spiritual leadership in your home to watch over you and to protect you from those who would lead you astray. Your church's pastor is also called to watch over and protect you. In Hebrews 13:17b, the King James Bible tells of the responsibility of pastors in this way, "For they watch for your souls, as they that must give account, that they may do it with joy, and not with grief: for that is unprofitable for you." That's why it's so important to be in church and hear the truth of God's Word taught. You also have a personal responsibility to read and know the Word for yourself.

Read about Paul's concerns and how he had to defend himself again against false accusations in 2 Corinthians 11:1–15.

### Discussion and Notebook Work

1. Use your Bible dictionary-concordance to record the definition for *deceive*. Read the related Scriptures.

2. Look back over today's portion of Scripture to learn the three ways Paul identified false apostles and record them in a sentence.

3. Record and answer reason questions.
   a. How did Paul refute his critics concerning his apostleship?
   b. How can you guard yourself against false teachers and keep yourself from turning away from the Gospel?

# Mapping Paul's Journeys
## Acts 27–28

You may remember reading the Scriptures referring to what Christians call the Great Commission. To review, Jesus speaks to the disciples in Matthew 28:18b–20a saying, "All authority in heaven and on earth has been given to me. Therefore go and make disciples of all nations, baptizing them in the name of the Father and of the Son and of the Holy Spirit, and teaching them to obey everything I have commanded you." Mark 16:15b repeats the message in this way, "Go into all the world and preach the good news to all creation." Jesus restated the Great Commission after the crucifixion and before He ascended into heaven in Acts 1:8, "But you will receive power when the Holy Spirit comes on you; and you will be my witnesses in Jerusalem, and in all Judea and Samaria, and to the ends of the earth." We see this happening in Acts and particularly in the missionary journeys of Paul. Each of Paul's missionary journeys took the Gospel farther and farther from Jerusalem as he endeavored to obey the leading of the Holy Spirit and the Word of God. Refer to the map of Paul's journeys in *The Children's Illustrated Bible* on page 297 or other maps provided by your teacher to help you visualize this very important aspect of New Testament history.

### Discussion and Notebook Work

1. Practice and recite the Great Commission.

"And Jesus came and spake unto them, saying, All power is given unto me in heaven and in earth. Go ye therefore, and teach all nations, baptizing them in the name of the Father, and of the Son, and of the Holy Ghost: Teaching them to observe all things whatsoever I have commanded you; and, lo, I am with you always, even unto the end of the world." (Matthew 28:18–20)

2. Complete the reading of Acts twenty-seven and twenty-eight to learn of Paul's trip to Rome and to learn the exciting details of his trip.

3. Follow your teacher's instructions to complete a map showing the four journeys of Paul. Use a different colored pencil for each journey. This work will take you several class periods. These journeys are described in the following passages:

* First journey, Acts 13:4–14:28
* Second journey, Acts 15:39–18:22
* Third journey, Acts 18:23–21:17
* Fourth journey, Acts 27:1–28:16

Oh, child of God, you've come a long way on your journey through Scripture from the creation of the world to the Acts of the Apostles and the newly formed church. Hopefully, you have learned something about what it means to walk with Jesus. However, the truth is you've only received a drop from the ocean of knowledge there is to be learned from reading God's Word. Like the teaching in Isaiah 28, this knowledge only comes "precept upon precept; line upon line, line upon line, here a little, and there a little" as our understanding grows to comprehend the God who created the universe.

I pray you will make it a lifelong pursuit to know God and how to walk with Him. Be assured that He wants your fellowship and desires to be your closest Friend. His Word says in Jeremiah 29:13–14, "You will seek me and find me when you seek me with all your heart. I will be found by you." As you read His Word, pray, and apply what you've learned, you will hear His voice speak to you words of comfort, words of direction, and whatever you need at that moment. Remember, He is not just the God of the Bible: He is the God of eternity and He is with you even as you read this page. And if you choose to continue walking with Jesus, He will lead you on the adventure of a lifetime.

*Barbara Keller*